Introduction

A: Legal and management

B: Health and welfare

C: General safety

D: High risk activities

E: Environment

Contents

F: Specialist activities

Further information

Introduction

Overview

The purpose of this book is to explain the basic health, safety and environmental steps that you, your employer and the site or project that you are working on should be taking.

The content provides easy to understand information, practical guidance and each chapter starts with a summary of what sites and employers should do for you, as well as what they expect from you.

It has been written to assist operatives and specialists sitting the CITB *Health, safety and environment test*, which is a key requirement when obtaining a construction industry competency card.

The content follows the new test structure (for tests taken from April 2012).

GE 707 is also the official supporting document for the CITB Site Safety Plus one-day health and safety awareness course.

Feedback

If you have any comments on the content, suggestions for improvement or additional topics your feedback would be very welcomed. You can contact us by:

 publications@citb.co.uk

 0344 994 4122.

A message from the Health and Safety Executive

A competent workforce is needed to reduce accidents and ill health arising from work in the construction industry.

The *Health, safety and environment test* will help workers in construction to become competent at identifying health and safety risks on site. This *Safe start* publication provides a reference source for the *Health, safety and environment test* as well as a standalone guide.

Workers in construction need to participate in improving health and safety standards on site. By contributing to the consultation process with their employer and with principal contractors, workers can help to prevent dangerous conditions from developing on site.

Workers in construction need to develop their skills in identifying risks and be confident in speaking out when seeing something wrong.

About the construction industry

Approximately 2.47 million people are employed in the UK construction industry.

It includes housing, utilities, repair and maintenance, refurbishment, shopfitting, demolition, roofing, mechanical and electrical, plumbing and highways maintenance.

It is made up of 197,965 construction businesses and 90% of companies employ less than 10 workers.

Construction workers (just like you) could die due to work-related ill health if control measures are not followed.

Work-related respiratory disease covers a range of illnesses that are caused or made worse by breathing in hazardous substances (such as construction dust) that damage the lungs.

4,500 people die each year due to past exposure to asbestos.

500 (and more each year) are dying from silica-related lung diseases (dust from cutting blocks, kerbs, and so on). Many more suffer from occupational asthma or are forced to leave the industry due to work-related ill health.

For 2013 there was an estimated 31,000 new cases of work-related ill health, with rates of musculoskeletal disorder significantly higher than average.

On average 50 workers are killed each year due to accidents. The biggest killer (around half) is due to falls from height.

Each year approximately 2,500 are seriously injured (broken bones, fractured skull, amputations, and so on) and 5,700 have reportable injuries.

The most common reported injuries are due to manual handling, slips, trips and falls and being struck by moving or falling objects.

60% of all work at height injuries are due to falls from below head height.

Setting out

Construction is an exciting industry. It is constantly changing as projects move on and jobs get done. As a result of this a building site is one of the most dangerous environments to work in.

But many accidents that occur on sites can be avoided if everyone on site works together. So a free film *Setting out* sets out what the site must do, and what you must do to stay healthy and safe at work.

 Setting out is available from www.citb.co.uk

This film is essential viewing for everyone involved in construction, and should be viewed before sitting the CITB *Health, safety and environment test*. The content of the film is captured in summary here, and these principles form the basis for the case studies, which were included in the test from Spring 2012.

Part 1: What you should expect from the construction industry

Your site and your employer should be doing all they can to keep you and your colleagues safe.

Before any work begins the site management team will have been planning and preparing the site for your arrival. It is their job to ensure that you can do your job safely and efficiently.

Five things the site you are working on must do:

- ☑ know when you are on site (signing in and out)
- ☑ give you a site induction
- ☑ give you site specific information
- ☑ encourage communication
- ☑ keep you up to date and informed.

Part 2: What the industry expects of you

Once the work begins, it is up to every individual to take responsibility for carrying out the plan safely.

This means you should follow the rules and guidelines as well as being alert to the continuing changes on site.

Five things you must do:

- ☑ respect and follow the site rules
- ☑ safely prepare each task
- ☑ do each task responsibly
- ☑ know when to stop (if you think anything is unsafe)
- ☑ keep learning.

Every day the work we do improves the world around us. It is time for us to work together to build an industry that puts its people first. By working together we can build a better industry that respects those who work in it.

Working well together

working well together

The working well together (WWT) campaign is an industry led initiative that helps support micro and small businesses improve their health and safety performance. The campaign undertakes a variety of activities including health and safety awareness days, designer awareness days, breakfast and evening events, roadshows and regional WWT groups.

"EVERY WEEK ONE OF US DIES"

To find out how the WWT campaign can help you and your company, go to wwt.uk.com

How to use Safe start

GE 707 follows the standard structure that is used across all core CITB publications:

Section A: Legal and management

Section B: Health and welfare

Section C: General safety

Section D: High risk activities

Section E: Environment

Each chapter begins with a summary list of what your site and employer should do together with a corresponding checklist for what you should do for your site and employer.

Use of icons

A set of icons emphasises important points within the text and also directs readers to further information. The icons are explained below.

 Website/further info

 Important

 Case study

 Example

 Good practice

 Quote

 Question

 Poor practice

 Definition

 Ideas

 Caution

 Checklist

 Notes

 Consultation

Video

 Favourite

Guidance

Augmented reality

What is augmented reality?

Augmented reality (AR) is cutting-edge technology. It provides layers of digital information (videos, photographs, sounds) simply by downloading an app and using the camera and sensors in your smartphone or tablet.

This technology has been used to connect you with additional and complementary content. This can be accessed via your mobile device when you install the Layar app.

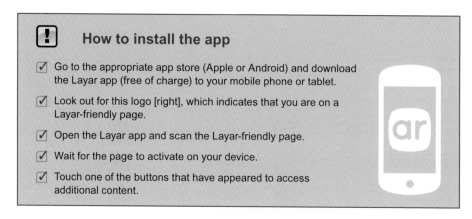

[!] How to install the app

☑ Go to the appropriate app store (Apple or Android) and download the Layar app (free of charge) to your mobile phone or tablet.

☑ Look out for this logo [right], which indicates that you are on a Layar-friendly page.

☑ Open the Layar app and scan the Layar-friendly page.

☑ Wait for the page to activate on your device.

☑ Touch one of the buttons that have appeared to access additional content.

01
General responsibilities

A
01

What your site and employer should do for you

1. Provide a safe place to work.

2. Provide a safe method of work and safe equipment.

3. Tell you about the hazards and how the risks should be controlled.

4. Provide training and information so you can do your job safely.

5. Communicate with you and allow you to have your say.

What you should do for your site and employer

1. Attend and participate in safety inductions and briefings.

2. Follow the site rules and your safe system of work.

3. Avoid taking short cuts or risks.

4. Report anything which you think is unsafe.

5. Co-operate and get involved.

Introduction

Everyone at work has a responsibility for health and safety, both morally and legally.

By knowing what is required, you will be able to understand what you and your employer's legal duties are to protect your safety and health while at work.

A
01

This chapter will help you understand:

- ☑ what the law requires everyone to do
- ☑ that employers must provide places of work that are safe for everyone
- ☑ that safe systems of work must be planned and put in place
- ☑ that the people involved need to be competent and trained
- ☑ that communication has to be effective so everyone knows what is expected
- ☑ that the Health and Safety Executive can enforce the law.

What the law requires

The Health and Safety at Work Act 1974 was introduced to protect the health and safety of everyone at work.

It means every employer must provide:

- ☑ a safe and healthy place to work
- ☑ safe ways of working
- ☑ tools, plant and equipment that are safe to use
- ☑ suitable training and adequate supervision
- ☑ means to communicate information and instructions.

It also means **you** also have a **legal duty** to comply with your employer in all matters of health and safety.

Providing safe ways of working

The law requires employers to put in place safe systems of work.

These are basically made up of:

- ☑ a health and safety policy
- ☑ method statements
- ☑ risk assessments
- ☑ permits to work.

A
01

Health and safety policy

Your employer's policy:

☑ will show you how health and safety is managed in your company

☑ should identify what the arrangements are (how and what should be done)

☑ show who is responsible for what (including **you**).

Method statements explain how the job is to be done safely and identify:

☑ the materials and equipment to be used

☑ the people and skills required

☑ the sequence, method and controls to be followed.

Risk assessments explain:

☑ the hazards of the job (for example an open excavation)

☑ the risks (for example persons falling in)

☑ the controls needed to minimise the risk to a safe level (for example erect double handrail around all sides of excavation).

Permit to work

☑ A system for controlling activities that are deemed high risk or need extra controls, (such as hot-work permits, permits to dig, confined space entry permits).

☑ A permit has strict controls and limitations which must be followed.

☑ You must never start any job for which a permit is required before the permit's start time and before the permit controls are in place.

[?] **Do you follow a safe system of work?**

Are you familiar with your safe system of work? Do you know what the sequence and hazards are and do you have the right equipment and training?

Do you fully understand the identified control measures? Or are you doing it the way you have always done the job, the way you think it should be done or just having to make do with what you have got?

If you are working differently from the safe system of work written down then speak to your supervisor or employer. Your way may well be better, quicker or more efficient but it may have additional or different risks that your employer hasn't thought about. These will need to be assessed and if necessary extra controls can then be put in place.

People need to be trained and competent

The law requires that everyone needs to be competent to either plan, manage or carry out work safely.

Competence is a mixture of:

- ☑ training
- ☑ knowledge
- ☑ experience.

You should never be put in a position where you are required to carry out a job for which you are not competent.

If you feel you are, then you may be putting yourself or others at risk – you need to speak to your supervisor or the site manager.

Sharing information and knowledge

Good communication of health and safety information is essential for everyone.

Employers have a legal duty to consult with their workforce. To be effective it needs to be two way (listen to as well as talk to).

This can be done in a variety of ways, such as:

- ☑ site inductions
- ☑ toolbox talks
- ☑ safety briefings
- ☑ worker involvement schemes
- ☑ informal chats/open door policies
- ☑ posters
- ☑ suggestion boxes.

Site induction

It is important that you attend a site induction for each new site that you go on. As a minimum you should be told about:

- ☑ the site rules
- ☑ welfare facilities
- ☑ emergency and first-aid arrangements
- ☑ where you will be working
- ☑ areas of the site you can and cannot go
- ☑ the current site hazards.

Toolbox talks

These are short health and safety briefing sessions on a particular subject connected to the work being carried out.

A toolbox talk should give you the opportunity to ask questions or raise concerns.

The aim of a toolbox talk is to give and share information to help keep you safe and protect your health.

Worker involvement

Many sites and employers realise that the workers are often the best people to understand the risks in their workplace. Talking to, listening and co-operating with each other can help:

☑ identify joint solutions to problems

☑ raise standards

☑ reduce accidents and ill health

☑ you and your workmates to do their job.

 Have your say

Sites run suggestion schemes, regular safety forum/meetings and open door policies.

Please get involved – your views are important and can make a difference.

How the Health and Safety Executive enforces the law

The Health and Safety Executive (HSE) is a Government body responsible for overseeing most aspects of workplace health and safety in the UK.

The HSE's main roles are to:

☑ offer advice on workplace health and safety

☑ carry out workplace inspections

☑ conduct serious accident investigations

☑ carry out enforcement action for health and safety breaches.

The HSE:

☑ has the legal power to demand entry to the workplace without notice

☑ can prosecute a company, an employer or an individual employee

☑ can issue improvement notices or prohibition notices which must be obeyed.

Improvement notices

These are issued if something is unsafe, not up to standard or not being adequately controlled.

They will state how the law was being broken and give a date by which things must be put right or improved.

Prohibition notices

These are issued when something is so unsafe all work connected to it must **stop** immediately.

Work must **not** start again until the matter has been put right.

02

Accident recording and reporting

A 02

What your site and employer should do for you

1. Listen, and ensure any concerns you have are acted on.

2. Put measures in place that allow different trades to work safely together.

3. Encourage accidents and near misses to be reported.

4. Provide an accident book and ensure records are kept.

5. Ensure accident investigations are carried out to understand what went wrong so they can be prevented from happening again (and not to find someone to blame).

What you should do for your site and employer

1. Understand and follow your safe system of work.

2. Stop and take advice if you need to change your safe system of work.

3. Report any accident you have and enter it into the accident book.

4. Report any near misses or anything you think could be unsafe.

5. Co-operate with any investigation.

Introduction

 On average 50 construction workers are killed each year due to accidents.

The biggest cause of fatalities is **falls from height.**

Each year approximately **2,500** are **seriously injured** (broken bones, fractured skull, amputations, and so on) and **5,700** have **reportable injuries.**

60% of all work at height injuries are due to **falls from below head height.**

A
02

Year after year the same types of accidents and incidents are repeated.

Common types of accident and incident

☑ Falling from height.

☑ Slips and trips.

☑ Manual handling.

☑ Being struck by mobile plant.

☑ Trapped in an excavation.

☑ Exposure to hazardous substances.

In many cases these could have been avoided by taking simple precautionary measures.

Prevention – what you can do

☑ Ensure you fully understand the safe system of work.

☑ Work to the instructions you are given.

☑ Follow the site rules.

☑ Do not be tempted to take risky short cuts.

☑ Keep your work area tidy.

☑ Keep access routes and walkways clear of materials and equipment.

☑ Report anything you think may be unsafe to your supervisor.

Accidents

A
02

You must ensure that any accident or injury you have is reported and recorded in the accident book.

Details that **must** be recorded in the accident book are:

- ☑ the injured person's name and address
- ☑ the injured person's occupation
- ☑ date and time of the accident
- ☑ where the accident happened
- ☑ how the accident happened
- ☑ details of the person filling in the book (if different from the injured person).

If you witness an accident it is important you tell your supervisor or employer.

By reporting accidents lessons can be learnt that may prevent them from happening again.

More serious accidents and those that result in more than seven days off work have to be reported by your employer to the HSE.

Near misses

An incident that nearly resulted in an injury or damage

Unsafe conditions

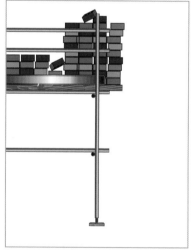

Something with the potential to cause harm

Unfortunately, not enough near misses or unsafe conditions are reported.

You may think reporting them will get you into trouble – but the opposite is true:

☑ each one is a potential learning event

☑ reporting them really can help to prevent accidents from happening.

A
02

Accident reporting and recording

A
02

03

Emergency procedures and first aid

A
03

What your site and employer should do for you

1. Inform you, at site induction, of the first aid and emergency procedures.

2. Have emergency information, contacts and telephone numbers displayed.

3. Provide emergency and rescue equipment.

4. Provide first aiders or first-aid procedures.

5. Maintain emergency escape routes and equipment.

What you should do for your site and employer

1. Know how to raise the alarm.

2. Know what to do in an emergency or site evacuation.

3. Be aware of the emergency procedures relating to your own safe system of work.

4. Know where and how to get first aid.

5. Know where to assemble in case of emergency.

Introduction

Every site should have emergency procedures in place in case of an emergency, such as:

☑ fire

☑ collapse

☑ persons trapped or needing rescue

☑ serious injury

☑ chemical spill.

A
03

You must know:

☑ how to raise the alarm

☑ what the alarm sounds or looks like

☑ the safe method or route of escape/evacuation

☑ where to assemble.

Information should be given during site induction and displayed on noticeboards or signs.

Remember – sites are constantly changing and so can emergency escape routes.

 Make sure you always know where your escape routes (and any equipment you may need) are.

You should also be familiar with any emergency procedures that form part of your method statement (such as confined space entry and rescue from height).

First aid

Site induction

During your site induction you should be told:

☑ who the first aider is

☑ how to find, contact or recognise them (for example green hat or sticker on hard hat)

☑ where to get first aid

☑ where the first-aid kit is located.

The aim of first aid is to:

☑ preserve life

☑ make sure the emergency services are called for immediately if required

☑ stop the casualty getting worse.

A
03

What employers must provide

Accidents and injuries do happen on site and employers must provide:

☑ trained people (such as first aiders) to respond to an incident

☑ the correct type of first-aid equipment for the hazards (for example, eyewash and burns kits)

☑ arrangements for lone workers or when the first aider is not there.

They should also take into account how far the site is from a hospital or the emergency services.

First aiders

There are two types of training for first aiders at work:

☑ first aider – trained in first aid for the workplace including life-saving techniques

☑ appointed person – trained in basic life-saving techniques.

Discovering a casualty

What you can do

If you are first on the scene of an accident your actions could be crucial.

You should do the following:

☑ **make sure you do not put yourself in danger**

☑ assess the situation

☑ if it is safe to do so remove or isolate the hazard

☑ go to the casualty and find out what's wrong

☑ **call for help** – if no-one comes go and find help and call the emergency services

☑ return and stay with the casualty until help arrives.

It is crucial that time is not wasted. The priority is getting assistance (first aider) or the emergency services to the injured person as soon as possible.

04

Health and welfare

What your site and employer should do for you
1. Identify work activities that could damage your health.
2. Tell you about the hazards and how the risks should be controlled.
3. Provide safe methods and equipment to minimise any exposure.
4. Provide you with free personal protective equipment (PPE).
5. Provide good, clean welfare facilities.

B
04

What you should do for your site and employer
1. Understand how the hazards can damage your long-term health.
2. Follow the safe system of work.
3. Wear your personal protective equipment (PPE).
4. Do not misuse the welfare facilities and help keep them clean and tidy.
5. Ask if in any doubt and report any changes in your health.

Introduction

Work-related ill health has devastating consequences for individuals and their families but it is very much misunderstood and underestimated.

This is because the effects of exposure to most work-related ill health hazards are not immediate or not even felt (unlike an accident which causes injury). You may go home from work feeling more or less the same each day and are none the wiser.

As you are repeatedly exposed to small doses of dust and fumes they start to damage your body. It can take many weeks, months or even years before symptoms of exposure become a problem to you and irreversible damage may well have occurred.

B
04

The common causes of work-related ill health

Noise and vibration

Refer to Chapter B07 for information on noise and vibration.

Respiratory (breathing) diseases

Refer to Chapter B06 for information on respiratory diseases.

Skin conditions

Dermatitis

This is a skin condition that is generally caused by exposure to chemicals and other harmful substances. Hands and forearms are most affected. It can be extremely painful and will affect your personal life as well as work life.

Symptoms include:

- ☑ redness
- ☑ itching
- ☑ dryness
- ☑ cracking or blistering.

Allergic dermatitis can make your skin so sensitive you will not be able to use some substances again.

Skin cancer

The number of skin cancer cases continues to increase every year. Those who work outdoors are at greater risk.

To prevent overexposure:

- ☑ cover up with loose clothing
- ☑ use sun block on exposed arms, face and neck.

It is vital that you drink plenty of water to prevent dehydration.

 If you notice new moles or changes to existing moles seek medical advice as soon as possible. Don't ignore it – early treatment is vital.

Less common is skin cancer caused by skin contact with mineral oils. Daily contact with items (such as oily clothing or gloves) can lead to a form of skin cancer. Mineral oils are common on mechanical plant and pipe threading machines.

Diseases carried in the blood

B 04

Leptospirosis (Weil's disease)

This disease:

☑ is carried by **rats** or **dairy cattle**

☑ enters the bloodstream through cuts and grazes

☑ is a particular problem when working on or near water, sewage, waterlogged sites or rat infested areas.

Minimise risk by:

☑ wearing appropriate gloves

☑ keeping all cuts and grazes covered with a waterproof plaster

☑ washing your hands before eating or smoking.

Wherever possible discourage rats from coming onto site by putting all food waste in covered bins.

 The early symptoms are often like the flu. If left untreated the disease may lead to kidney problems and can be fatal.

Tetanus (lockjaw)

☑ This is a disease of the nervous system.

☑ It enters the body through cuts, grazes or puncture wounds.

☑ Germs are found in contaminated soils or manure.

☑ An early symptom is an increasing difficulty in opening the mouth or jaw.

Hepatitis

☑ Hepatitis is usually caught from contact with infected needles and syringes.

  – If you find any suspected drug taking equipment leave it alone.

  – Contact your supervisor or employer.

Legionella

This is a form of pneumonia, which is caught from:

☑ bacteria found in warm, damp places such as:
  - air conditioning/hot water systems, cooling towers

☑ breathing in contaminated water vapour/mist.

A safe system of work is required if legionella is suspected.

Drugs and alcohol

B
04

Anyone caught working under the influence of illegal drugs or alcohol will have to leave site immediately and could lose their job.

Many employers and clients have policies to carry out random testing for drugs and alcohol as well as for cause (if suspected or involved in an accident).

Prescribed drugs

☑ Over-the-counter and prescription drugs can have side effects.

☑ You should read the label or speak to the pharmacist if in doubt.

☑ Some hay fever medicines can make you drowsy, which could mean you are not safe to be on a construction site or fit to drive.

Illegal drugs

People under the influence of illegal drugs are a danger to themselves and everyone else on site. They are likely to suffer from:

☑ Poor or irrational decision making   ☑ Clumsiness

☑ Slow reaction times   ☑ Distorted vision.

The effects and traces of some drugs can stay in your system for prolonged periods (for example cannabis can be detected during testing several weeks or even months after it has been taken). Unlike alcohol, there are no permitted safe levels for illegal drugs so a trace could mean failing a drugs test.

Alcohol

Depending upon your employer or site policy the blood alcohol level required to pass a test can be a third of the current legal driving limit.

Besides being a danger to themselves and others, anyone still under the influence of alcohol at work risks losing their job and livelihood. Of those that are convicted of drink driving, many were driving the morning after a few drinks the night before. Most underestimate the length of time it takes to sober up.

The effects of alcohol can last for hours

On average it takes one hour for your body to get rid of one unit of alcohol.

A unit is the volume (litres) x ABV (% strength), for example:

☑ One litre of 5% lager   = 1 x 5   = five units (one pint = 2.8 units)

☑ 750 ml bottle of 12% wine   = 0.75 x 12   = nine units

☑ 750 ml bottle of 40% whisky   = 0.75 x 40   = 30 units.

15 units = six pints of lager or half a bottle of whisky.

If starting at 7 pm and drinking five pints it could be up to 10 am the next morning before all the alcohol is out of your system.

B
04

Welfare facilities

Your employer has a legal duty to provide adequate welfare facilities that include:

☑ an adequate number of toilets

☑ hand-washing facilities

☑ changing and drying rooms where necessary

☑ somewhere to take breaks from work

☑ chairs with back support (not canteen benches)

☑ a supply of clean drinking water

☑ a means of boiling water for drinks

☑ a facility to warm up food (for example a microwave)

☑ a means to secure valuables and change of clothes (for example lockers).

Hand-washing facilities (not the canteen sink) must include:

☑ a supply of running hot (or warm) and cold water

☑ soap or hand cleaner

☑ a way of hygienically drying your hands.

Welfare facilities must be kept clean and in good order. If they are not, then speak to your supervisor or the person responsible.

 Welfare facilities are provided for your benefit – please look after them.

05

Personal protective equipment

What your site and employer should do for you

1. Identify risks and eliminate them where possible.

2. Where there is still a risk, personal protective equipment (PPE) which protects you from those risks must be provided.

3. Supply PPE free of charge.

4. Provide facilities to clean, store and maintain PPE.

5. Show you how and where to use and care for PPE.

B
05

What you should do for your site and employer

1. Wear your PPE at all times when required.

2. Wear the right PPE for the task.

3. Put it on and adjust it so it fits right..

4. Look after and care for your PPE.

5. Report any PPE defects.

Introduction

PPE consists of items and clothing designed to protect you from a variety of hazards.

Your employer must:

☑ carry out a risk assessment and write a method statement to identify any hazards and risks, and what can be done to eliminate or control them

☑ supply you with PPE whenever there is a hazard that cannot be eliminated or minimised to a safe level

☑ supply PPE free of charge.

 PPE should only be used as a last resort.

Policies and site rules

Some sites have mandatory PPE policies or rules, which include the use of gloves and eye protection. This is because:

☑ you can be exposed to a variety of hazards and risks

☑ hazards and risks can change daily and can be outside the control of you or your employer.

On most sites you can only take off PPE when you are in a safe area (such as the site office and welfare compound).

Common examples of PPE are:

☑ safety helmets (hard hats)

☑ safety footwear/boots

☑ high-visibility clothing

☑ safety glasses (light eye protection)

☑ gloves.

There are times when you will need to wear other additional PPE when required by:

☑ a risk assessment or method statement

☑ instructions from your supervisor or employer

☑ site rules/site induction

☑ signs and notices.

Other task – specific PPE includes:

- ☑ impact goggles*
- ☑ ear defenders (muffs) and earplugs
- ☑ respirators and face masks
- ☑ full face shields

- ☑ safety harnesses and lanyards
- ☑ knee pads, overalls
- ☑ wet weather clothing
- ☑ lifejackets or buoyancy aids.

Safety glasses or light eye protection (LEP) are not designed for tasks where impact goggles should be worn (such as using cartridge tools, grinders, disc cutters).

Your employer must provide PPE, but you must:

- ☑ take care of your PPE (keep it clean and inspect it regularly)
- ☑ use your PPE as instructed
- ☑ **not** work without it where it is required
- ☑ stop work and report any lost or damaged PPE to your supervisor.

B
05

Types of personal protective equipment

Head protection

On most sites safety helmets must be worn at all times, except when you are in a safe area.

A safety helmet is worn to protect you from falling objects or bumping your head. To be effective a safety helmet must be:

- ☑ worn the right way round (peak at the front)
- ☑ adjusted so it fits snug and square on your head
- ☑ fitted with a chin strap if there is a risk of it falling off while working
- ☑ fitted with a proprietary liner for cold weather (not wearing it over your woolly hat).

Do not cut, drill holes, paint or apply unauthorised stickers to your safety helmet, as this can severely reduce its capacity to protect you in an incident.

Dropping your safety helmet from height onto a hard surface can also reduce the strength, even if there is no obvious damage. If this happens it should be replaced.

Foot protection

Safety footwear must:

- ☑ be worn at all times on site
- ☑ have protective toe-caps.

Some types:

- ☑ have a steel mid-sole to protect from puncture injuries (standing on a nail)
- ☑ offer better ankle support

☑ offer good grip on sloping roofs or slippery surfaces (such as safety trainers)

☑ offer increased comfort and are more suitable to trades (such as floor layers) who repeatedly kneel and bend their feet.

High-visibility clothing

☑ All personnel and visitors on site should wear a high-visibility vest or coat as a minimum.

☑ There are three classes of high-visibility clothing:
  - **Class 1 – low visibility** suitable for general sites
  - **Class 2 – medium visibility** required when working on or near A and B class roads or heavily trafficked sites
  - **Class 3 – high visibility** required when working on or near dual carriageways, motorways, airports, railways (same reflective strips as Class 2 but with long sleeves).

B
05

Body protection

Protective clothing can protect against:

☑ strong oils and chemicals (cement)

☑ fire hazards

☑ rough or sharp surfaces

☑ extreme cold or heat

☑ weather.

Hearing protection

There are two main types:

☑ ear defenders or earmuffs – these have to be a snug fit to be effective

☑ earplugs:
  - make sure your earplugs are inserted deeply enough
  - if they feel loose or fall out then they are not inserted correctly
  - do not reuse disposable earplugs, which can cause infection.

Eye and face protection

There are three main types, shown below.

Safety goggles

Safety glasses (light eye protection)

Full face shield

- ☑ Eye protection protects against:
  - – flying debris and objects
  - – chemical splashes
  - – airborne dust
  - – molten metal and sparks.
- ☑ Eye protection needs to be regularly cleaned and stored to protect from scratching.
- ☑ You need to see through a pair of goggles to work safely.
- ☑ If your eye protection is scratched or keeps misting up then you need a suitable replacement.

Safety glasses are only classed as light eye protection and will not withstand an impact from flying debris when using grinders, disc cutters, cartridge tools, and so on.

B 05

Respiratory protective equipment

To prevent exposure to harmful dust, fibres and fumes, employers must provide you with the correct type of respiratory (breathing) protective equipment (RPE).

- ☑ Where dust cannot be avoided you must wear suitable RPE (masks).
- ☑ If wearing any mask it should have a BS EN number and/or CE mark printed on it.
- ☑ Disposable masks should have at least two adjustable straps and a flexible nose band to shape around the bridge of your nose.

Cheap disposable dust masks from DIY stores offer little or no protection.

Other types are half face or full face respirators with replacement filter cartridges.

- ☑ All masks have a filter rating FFP3, FFP2 or FFP1.
- ☑ The filters can protect against different hazards (such as dusts or vapours).
- ☑ Generally speaking:
  - – FFP3 will offer the maximum protection, especially against vapours and fumes
  - – FFP2 are good for medium risk (such as wood dust or concrete cutting)
  - – FFP1 for light duty work (such as sweeping up).

Your risk or COSHH assessment should state what type of filter you need. As a rule of thumb disposable respirator masks are designed for an eight-hour shift.

If in any doubt – ask. You have the right not to breathe in harmful dusts and fumes.

Protect today – breathe easily tomorrow.

Refer to Chapter B05 for further guidance.

Hand and skin protection

☑ Gloves should be suitable for the hazards and task. Using the correct type of gloves will protect your hands.

☑ If using chemicals the gloves should be impervious (the chemical should not be absorbed by the glove and inside onto your hands).

☑ It is important gloves are regularly cleaned or replaced.

Barrier creams are no substitute for gloves but can offer an additional line of protection. Using hand soap, hand cleaners and after work creams to replace oils lost from your skin will help in prevention.

Never use solvents or spirits to clean your hands. These strip the protective oils from your hands leaving you more prone to attack. 5%–10% of construction workers working with cement, mortar and concrete are affected by dermatitis.

B
05

Flotation equipment

If you have to work near or over water where there is a risk of drowning, you should be provided with a buoyancy aid (such as a lifejacket). Wear it at all times.

Falling in while wearing your work clothing and boots, and even tool belts will drag you under or sap your energy very quickly, especially in cold water.

Self-inflating lifejackets automatically inflate and turn you onto your back if you fall in, even if you are unconscious, allowing you to breathe.

Other, more basic but equally important equipment (such as life-buoys, life-rings or throwing lines) may also be provided.

Where strong currents or fast flowing water are present there may be a need for other equipment (such as manned rescue boats).

Personal protective equipment

B
05

06

Dust and fumes (Respiratory risks)

What your site and employer should do for you

1. Ensure that dust, fumes and vapours are either eliminated or minimised.

2. Ensure that information about asbestos is made available to the workforce and others who may be affected.

3. Provide systems and equipment to ensure that airborne dust, fumes and vapours are minimised to the lowest level.

4. Provide information and training on the hazards and controls (such as exhaust systems and wet cutting methods).

5. Issue and train you in the use of respiratory protective equipment (RPE) required to protect your health.

B
06

What you should do for your site and employer

1. Understand how the hazards can damage your long-term health.

2. Follow the safe system of work.

3. Wear your RPE.

4. Do not misuse the welfare facilities and help keep them clean and tidy.

5. Ask if in any doubt and report any changes in your health.

Introduction

Work-related respiratory disease covers a range of illnesses that are caused or made worse by breathing in hazardous substances (such as construction dust) that damage the lungs.

☑ 4,500 people die each year due to past exposure to asbestos.

☑ 500 people (and more each year) are dying from silica-related lung diseases (dust from cutting blocks, kerbs, and so on).

Many more workers suffer from occupational asthma or are forced to leave the industry due to work-related ill health.

This is because the effects of exposure to most work-related ill health hazards are not always immediate or not even felt (unlike an accident which causes injury). You may go home from work feeling more or less the same each day and are none the wiser.

B
06

As you are repeatedly exposed to small doses of dust and fumes they start to damage your body. It can take many weeks, months or even years before symptoms of exposure become a problem to you and by then irreversible damage may well have occurred.

At any one time there are far more people off work through occupational ill health than there are because of a work-related accident.

Exposure to everyday hazards, including wood dusts, flux, welding and cutting fumes, dusts, asbestos and many more everyday workplace materials and processes, cause ill health.

The breathing in of dusts and fumes, known as respiratory sensitisers, are likely to cause an allergic reaction.

As an industry we are exposed to many materials and products and are therefore exposed to particular dust hazards (such as asbestos, cement, stone, silica, lead, fillers, MDF, plastics, epoxys, and solvents).

Breathing in hazardous airborne contaminants can cause wheezing, coughing, breathlessness, bronchitis and other respiratory diseases, including various types of cancer.

Exposure to solvents, vapours and fumes can cause headaches, dizziness, sickness, lung problems and affect other parts of the body.

Stomach disorders may be brought on by the ingestion of the dust of some substances, due to eating food with dirty and contaminated hands, or simply eating in a dusty environment.

What are the hazards?

The main respiratory hazards that may be encountered on site are shown below.

☑ **Mists.** Tiny liquid droplets formed, for example, when spraying or using an aerosol – mists may be a combination of several hazardous substances.

☑ **Metal fumes.** These occur when metal is heated to high temperatures (such as during welding and gas cutting) – fumes contain minute metal particles that may remain in the air and be inhaled, for some time.

☑ **Gases.** Airborne at room temperature, these normally mix with the air that we breathe (for example propane, butane, acetylene, carbon monoxide, hydrogen sulphide) and can spread very quickly.

☑ **Vapours.** The gaseous state of substances that are liquids or solids at room temperature – they usually form when substances evaporate (for example, the vapour from glue, paint or solvent).

☑ **Dry pigeon droppings.** If disturbed, these can become a hazardous airborne dust that can cause a severe respiratory illness – if work is to be carried out in an area where pigeons have been nesting or congregating, the area must be thoroughly decontaminated first.

☑ **Dusts.** Produced when solid materials are broken down into finer particles – the longer that the dust stays in the air the easier it is to breathe in.

B
06

Dust is by far the most common hazard on site.

What is dust?

Dust can simply be described as particles in air. What it consists of is purely down to what material is being cut, sanded or drilled, as the physical action of your tools releases small parts of the material into the atmosphere.

The harm that it can do to you is dependant on what the material is – don't fall for the misconception that all dust is the same.

Common harmful materials

Common materials which can do particular harm are shown below.

☑ **Wood – hardwood, softwood and plywood** dust is a serious problem. It can cause allergic reactions or cause cancers in the nose and lungs. Softwood dust is known to cause sensitisation (a form of allergic reaction), whereas hardwood is a known carcinogen (it causes cancer).

☑ **MDF** is made from separated softwood fibres, hardwood fibres and glues. When cut it has a greater potential to form a particularly fine dust. This increases the likelihood of dangerous amounts being breathed in.

☑ **Stone, brick, block, sand and concrete** all contain a compound called silica. Very fine silica dust is created when concrete, bricks, blocks, tiles and stone is sanded, cut or drilled. Breathing fine dust of crystalline silica can lead to the development of silicosis. This is scarring of the lung tissue and can lead to breathing difficulties. Exposure to very high concentrations over a relatively short period of time can cause acute silicosis, resulting in rapidly progressive breathlessness and death within a few months.

Prevention

Here are some simple steps that should be taken to protect you and the people around you.

☑ **Avoid creating dust.** Choosing the right equipment or method of work can really protect workers' lungs and potentially eliminate the risk altogether. Pre-ordering sized materials rather than cutting them on site and using a block splitter rather than a disc cutter creates less dust and is quicker.

☑ **Stop the dust getting into the air.** If creating dust can't be eliminated then stopping and minimising dust being released should be the priority every time. This can be done in two ways:

- **dampening down or wet cutting.** This is the cheapest and most effective way. Water helps to form a slurry that prevents the **majority** of dust becoming airborne. Not only does it reduce what is breathed in, but it also has the benefit of less cleaning up afterwards. It is important to keep the flow constant while wet cutting or grinding and to dampen down before sweeping up

- **capturing the dust.** Some materials (such as wood) do not suit the use of water to suppress dusts so consider alternatives (such as dust extraction). When purchasing or hiring tools, ensure they have the facility to extract the dust, as this is the only effective way to capture the dust being released. Some tools are fitted with dust bags, but these can have limited efficiency and clog up easily. Always try to use a means that will remove the dust by suction and remember to regularly clean filters. Cleaning dust from work areas and tools is far better if a vacuum is used rather than sweeping with a brush.

B
06

☑ **Wear protection.** Even the best control measures won't prevent all dust being released, so respiratory protection equipment or dust masks must always be worn even if you are wet cutting or using extraction.

Respiratory protective equipment

The choice of respiratory protective equipment (RPE) will depend upon the nature of hazard from which protection is required. In many cases RPE will only protect against one type of hazard (for example dust or fumes).

A wide range of RPE is available and you should check with your supervisor that the RPE you have or need matches that in the risk assessment or method statement.

You should be shown how to put on, adjust and maintain any RPE. You should be given and pass a face-fit test to ensure your RPE fits and functions correctly.

If you wear more than one type of RPE your employer must arrange for each type to be face-fit tested, which must be carried out by a competent person.

RPE or masks are assigned three protection factor levels:

- [✓] **FFP1 or P1**   offers a protection factor of 4
- [✓] **FFP2 or P2**   offers a protection factor of 10
- [✓] **FFP3 or P3**   offers a protection factor of 20.

You should always wear a P2 or preferably a P3 mask as these offer better protection. Make sure you wear one with a tight seal against the face. Beards and stubble over one day of growth simply lift the mask off the face meaning dust can get inside the seal so be aware of this.

Disposable dust masks are only designed to be used for one shift or one day's use. Cheap masks with no filter rating (and usually with only one strap) offer little or no protection against microscopic hazardous dust.

B
06

07

Noise and vibration

Noise and vibration

What your site and employer should do for you

1. Assess if the noise your job makes could damage your hearing.

2. Tell you about and provide the controls and PPE you need if it does.

3. Enforce a hearing protection zone if a site is noisy from multiple trades.

4. Assess if the vibration your tools make could damage hands.

5. Tell you about the controls, including the safe daily trigger time.

B
07

What you should do for your site and employer

1. Wear your hearing protection when required.

2. Make sure you fit the hearing protection properly.

3. Do not exceed the daily safe time limits for each tool.

4. Report any symptoms of hand-arm vibration syndrome (HAVS) if you think you have them.

5. Understand that any damage to your health will be permanent.

Noise – what's the problem?

Damage caused to your hearing by loud noise can be permanent. Some people lose their hearing completely, others can suffer from a constant, high-pitched ringing or buzzing in the ears. There is no cure.

Noise induced hearing loss can build up over time. You may not notice the effects each day, but over a period of time your hearing can get worse from work noise.

☑ You may start to turn the TV up a bit more than you used to.

☑ You may start to struggle to hear conversations or parts of words.

Many things on site cause loud noise, such as:

☑ tools and equipment you use

☑ equipment others are using

☑ a build up of multiple noises.

Noise that damages your hearing can be:

☑ **continuous** (such as from a diesel generator or using a certain tool over long periods of time)

☑ **sudden peaks** of high noise levels from impacts (such as cartridge tools or a piling rig).

Early signs or symptoms are:

☑ temporary deafness

☑ ringing in the ears

☑ reduced hearing

☑ headaches.

What your employer should do

They have a legal duty to ensure your hearing is not damaged at work where possible by:

☑ using less noisy plant and equipment

☑ reducing or isolating the noise.

Where this is not possible then they should:

☑ inform you of the risks and noise levels

☑ provide information on how you should protect your hearing

☑ provide hearing protection.

Hearing protection – two main types

☑ Ear defenders or earmuffs

☑ Earplugs.

B
07

Hearing protection zones

☑ Some parts of a site can be loud enough to become a risk for everyone.

☑ Hearing protection zones are then set up.

☑ You must wear your hearing protection at all times until you leave the area.

You have a duty to:

☑ wear hearing protection when required

☑ look after the PPE issued to you

☑ get your PPE replaced if lost or damaged

☑ inform your employer if you think your hearing is being damaged.

B
07

Estimating noise levels

☑ Hearing protection must be worn when noise levels are above 85 dB (decibels).

☑ You may request hearing protection for noise above 80 dB.

☑ It is difficult to know what 85 dB sound like, but as a rule of thumb use the one metre and two metre rule.

– **One metre rule:** if you have to raise your voice or shout to someone only **one metre** away to be heard you **definitely should be wearing hearing protection.**

– **Two metre rule:** if you have to raise your voice or shout to someone **two metres** away to be heard you **should be putting your hearing protection on.**

 Third rule – if in doubt, put your hearing protection on.

 Exposure times are lower than you might think

Electric hand tools are about 95 dB. The safe exposure time for this level of noise is only 15 minutes per day. After that you are at risk of permanent hearing damage.

A petrol cut-off saw is about 105 dB. Without hearing protection safe exposure time is only two minutes per day.

Vibration – what's the problem?

Serious and permanent health problems can occur from prolonged use of tools and equipment that expose your hands to vibration.

☑ Compressed air and electrical tools all cause vibration.

☑ Generally, the longer you operate a tool that can harm you, the more likely you are to be harmed.

☑ Some tools vibrate more than others and are a greater risk.

Vibration can lead to a condition known as **hand-arm vibration syndrome (HAVS)** and health problems known as **vibration white finger.**

Early signs or symptoms are:

☑ temporary loss or feeling in fingers

☑ tingling in the fingers

☑ whitening of the skin (blanching), especially the fingertips.

Symptoms are often worse in the damp or cold.

The serious damage

☑ There are different stages of HAVS.

☑ It is vital you tell your employer if you have any signs.

☑ If you ignore the symptons you could end up with permanent damage.

☑ The vibration damages blood vessels, nerves, muscle fibre, bones and joints.

B
07

Vibration damage to the wrist and hands

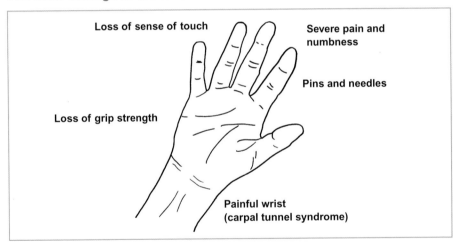

Damaged blood vessels = circulation problems resulting in:

☑ loss of movement or dexterity in your hands

☑ loss of sense of touch

☑ feeling of coldness

☑ almost permanent pins and needles

☑ at worst, ulceration or gangrene resulting in amputation.

Examples of vibratory equipment

☑ Compressed air breakers, rock drills, concrete pokers and scabblers.

☑ Hand-held electric drills and drill guns.

☑ Disc cutters, angle grinders, wall chasers.

☑ Sanders, circular saws, planers.

☑ Wacker plates, strimmers, jet washers.

**B
07**

What your employer should do

☑ Assess the risk.

☑ Put measures in place to ensure you are not exposed to harmful levels of vibration.

☑ Ensure you know the safe levels of exposure.

☑ Monitor your exposure.

☑ Make sure all vibratory tools and equipment are well maintained.

Safe usage time of equipment

☑ The safe usage time is the time the equipment is actually working.

☑ It is in effect the 'trigger time'.

☑ It is not the time spent doing the job.

Traffic light warning system

Some tools are now colour coded **green**, amber or **red**.

☑ **Green** = safely use eight hours per day.

☑ Amber = only use it part of the day.

☑ **Red** = high risk.

For amber and red labels you need to be told the specific daily safe exposure times.

What you have a duty to do

☑ Use the equipment only for as long as it is safe.

☑ Keep your hands warm.

☑ Relax your grip, as this can have a less harmful effect on your muscles.

Remember:

☑ that smokers can be more affected

☑ that anti-vibration gloves do not protect you

☑ to keep all points and chisels sharp.

08

Hazardous substances

Hazardous substances

What your site and employer should do for you

1. Use a less hazardous substance where possible.
2. Assess the risks of you using a substance.
3. Control exposure by providing a safe system of work.
4. Provide information and training on the risks and controls..
5. Monitor to make sure the controls are effective.

What you should do for your site and employer

1. Follow the safe system of work/controls (COSHH assessment).
2. Fully understand the hazards of using the substance.
3. Wear the correct PPE.
4. Inform the correct person of any incident or spill.
5. Store and dispose of the substance correctly.

B
08

What is a hazardous substance?

☑ Any substance that could harm your health (such as solvents, cement, asbestos).

☑ Any dust, fibres or fumes given off by a work process.

☑ Any substance that could harm the environment.

How can they affect your health?

☑ **Immediate** – burns to the skin from acids or chemicals.

☑ **Long-term** – developing cancer from asbestos exposure.

☑ **Disease** – contact with contaminated soil or water.

☑ **Sensitising** – over a period of time you start having more serious reactions to less and less exposure to the substance.

How do they get into your body?

☑ **Inhalation** – breathing in dust, fumes, vapours and fibres.

☑ **Absorption** – contact with your skin or open sores/wounds in your body.

☑ **Ingestion** – being swallowed or eaten (usually from holding food with dirty hands).

☑ **Injection** – needles, sharps or high pressure (such as water jetting).

What should your employer be doing?

Under The Control of Substances Hazardous to Health (COSHH) Regulations your employer should:

☑ use a less hazardous substance if available

☑ read and understand the manufacturer's information on the substance

☑ carry out a risk assessment on how and where it is to be used

☑ put in place measures to control the exposure

☑ make sure you know the controls

☑ monitor to make sure the controls are effective.

Some hazardous substances, such as fumes (welding), dust (cutting) or vapours (painting), do not have warning labels, as these are often created when you work.

 You employer has a legal duty to assess these hazards too, and complete a COSHH assessment as part of your safe system of work.

B
08

Identifying hazardous substances

The packaging or container will carry one or more symbol.

Danger

Very toxic or toxic

Substances that, in very low quantities or low quantities, cause death or acute or chronic damage to health when inhaled, swallowed or absorbed via skin.

Warning

Harmful

Substances that may cause death or acute or chronic damage to health when inhaled, swallowed or absorbed via skin.

Danger

Corrosive

Substances that may, on contact with living tissues, destroy them.

Warning

Irritant

Non-corrosive substances that may cause inflammation through immediate, prolonged or repeated contact with the skin or mucous membrane.

Danger

Disposal of hazardous substances

Hazardous substances can contaminate land, drains, sewers, rivers and the air.

You should **never**:

☑ mix with general (non-hazardous) waste

☑ pour down drains, sinks or onto the ground

☑ bury, burn or fly tip.

 Your site or employer should have a procedure to dispose of hazardous waste, including empty or part-used containers.

B
08

Common hazardous substances

Asbestos

Asbestos is a very harmful substance that continues to kill many people every year.

Microscopic asbestos fibres are invisible and are easily disturbed.

Breathing in **all** types of asbestos fibres can lead to lung diseases (such as mesothelioma, asbestosis and lung cancer).

 Any building constructed or refurbished before the year 2000 could contain asbestos.

An asbestos survey should be undertaken before work commences. There are two types of survey:

☑ management survey (to assess how to manage and protect asbestos in an occupied building)

☑ refurbishment or demolition survey (to find out if building work could disturb asbestos).

Asbestos can be correctly identified by getting a sample analysed in a laboratory.

You could come across asbestos if you are working on a building doing work such as:

☑ building an extension

☑ installing new plumbing, electrics, windows and soffits, loft insulation, kitchens and bathrooms

☑ modifying the structure

☑ refurbishment

☑ demolition and stripping out.

Where can you find asbestos?

- ☑ Asbestos cement roofing sheets, water tanks and pipes.
- ☑ Asbestos cement used as permanent formwork.
- ☑ Fly tipped/buried in the ground.
- ☑ Lagging of boilers, pipework or ducting.
- ☑ Pipework and boiler gaskets.
- ☑ Partitions and ceilings.
- ☑ Sprayed coatings to ceilings, columns and beams.
- ☑ Suspended ceiling tiles and floor tiles.
- ☑ Soffit panels and window boards.

B 08

If you think you have discovered, disturbed or drilled through asbestos:

- ☑ stop work immediately
- ☑ warn others nearby to keep away
- ☑ tell your supervisor or employer.

Asbestos removal

The removal of high risk asbestos containing materials (sprayed asbestos, asbestos lagging, asbestos insulating board) must be carried out by a licensed contractor.

The removal of low risk asbestos containing materials does not require a licence, providing that the correct precautions are taken (such as wearing the correct RPE).

Projects can be categorised as non-licensed work or notifiable non-licensed work. For notifiable non-licensed work there are additional duties for employers, such as ensuring that medical examinations are carried out and health records are maintained.

Lead

Lead is a cumulative poison that can find its way into the bloodstream and collect in tissues, particularly the bone marrow.

The ways that lead is likely to get into the body are through the:

☑ breathing in of fumes or dust

☑ ingestion of lead particles through hand to mouth contact.

Construction workers most at risk include those involved in:

☑ blast removal and burning of old lead paint

☑ stripping of old lead paint from doors and windows

☑ rubbing down or burning off old paintwork

☑ hot cutting in demolition and dismantling operations

☑ work on lead flashing, upstands and gutters

☑ handling old architectural lead work

☑ structural renovation or refurbishment, including conservation or heritage projects.

B
08

Control of exposure

Your employer must ensure that exposure to lead is either prevented or, where this is not reasonably practicable, adequately controlled by means of appropriate control measures.

Highly flammable liquids

Highly flammable liquids (HFLs) (such as thinners, solvents, petrol and adhesives) can easily catch fire and burn fiercely.

They can be identified by the following symbols.

If you have to use HFLs:

☑ check there are no naked flames or other sources of ignition nearby

☑ only take the amount needed with you

☑ always follow the storage procedures

☑ have the correct fire extinguisher at hand.

Liquid petroleum gas

Liquid petroleum gas (LPG) is a highly flammable gas. It is heavier than air so can sink into excavations, basements, drains, and so on.

It must be stored upright in a well-ventilated area and in a secure cage.

There are separate regulations covering the safe carrying of LPG bottles in vehicles.

LPG has a distinctive smell. If you think there might be a leak:

☑ warn others to evacuate the area

☑ if safe to do so:
  − turn off the supply valve on the cylinder
  − open doors and windows
  − eliminate any sources of ignition

☑ report it immediately.

Gas from a leaking LPG bottle can expand to 250 times its bottle volume. It can catch fire at some distance from the original leak.

B
08

09

Manual handling

What your site and employer should do for you

1. Identify work activities that pose a manual handling risk.

2. Provide safe methods and equipment to minimise the risk.

3. Tell you about the hazards and how the risks should be controlled.

4. Provide slip/trip free access routes and adequate lighting levels.

5. Help by planning delivery, off-loading and distribution of your materials and equipment to avoid unnecessary carrying and lifting.

B
09

What you should do for your site and employer

1. Follow the safe system of work.

2. Do not to put yourself at risk (both short and long-term).

3. Use lifting aids or techniques provided.

4. Get help (two person lift), split the load and do not carry too much.

5. Ask for advice if in doubt.

Introduction

 Manual handling is the moving of any load by hand, including lifting, putting down, pushing, pulling or carrying by hand or bodily force.

It is the construction industry's biggest cause of ill health.

Every year 90,000 workers are injured while manually handling loads.

Your back is very strong but **repeated** twisting, straining and incorrect lifting techniques can, over time, lead to an injury.

Manual handling injuries resulting from unsafe or incorrect manual handling can affect the:

☑ whole body

☑ back

☑ shoulders

☑ arms

☑ hands

☑ feet and ankles.

B
09

Back injuries are most common but hernias, ruptures, sprains and strains are all conditions that can result from manual handling.

Poor posture (such as slouching on the settee, sleeping on a poor supporting mattress, and sitting in a driving position that twists or doesn't support your spine) can all add to the problem.

Your employer has a legal duty to make sure that you are not required to carry out any manual handling activity that will harm you.

What your employer should do

☑ Identify the risks to your health that result from manual handling.

☑ Put measures in place to avoid manual handling where practicable.

☑ Carry out a risk assessment if it can't be avoided.

☑ Devise a way of moving the load so you are not injured.

☑ Tell you the safest method of moving the load.

☑ Provide any necessary equipment and training.

What you should do

☑ Follow the methods of working that will protect your health.

☑ Use any equipment that you have been given.

☑ Wear your personal protective equipment (PPE).

☑ Ask for advice if you are in doubt.

> The only way to avoid manual handling is to use mechanical handling equipment (such as cranes, forklifts, goods hoists and jacks).

Kinetic method of lifting

Bend at the knees (1)   *Grasp the load (2)*   *Lift, using the legs (3)*   *Carry the load (4)*

What should both you and your employer consider?

The task

☑ Can manual handling be avoided completely?

☑ Does the task involve repetitive lifting?

☑ Can the distance a load has to be moved be reduced? (Get it delivered or moved nearer).

☑ Can lifting aids be used (for example wheelbarrow, trolley, vacuum lifters)?

☑ How and from what height is the load to be lifted or lowered?

☑ Will it be necessary to over reach or stretch to put the load down?

☑ Does the task involve repetitive twisting while lifting a load?

The load

☑ Can the load be split down into smaller loads?

☑ Can it be moved by two (or more) people?

☑ Is the weight of the load known?

☑ Can it be gripped easily or are there adequate handholds?

☑ Centre of gravity – is the load top heavy or an uneven weight?

The individual

☑ Do they need any manual handling training or the technique for the equipment?

☑ Are they male or female, tall or small, young or old?

☑ Are there any previous injuries or health conditions?

The environment

☑ Is the floor or ground free from slip or trip hazards?

☑ Does the load need to be carried up steps or stairs?

☑ Are there any space constraints?

☑ Is the level of lighting adequate?

B
09

Manual handling

10

Safety signs and signals

What your site and employer should do for you

1. Ensure safety signs follow standard designs (not handwritten signs).

2. Maintain signs and make them clearly visible.

3. Provide signs that are appropriate to the hazard or risk.

4. Remove signs if they are no longer needed.

5. Display any safety sign identified in your safe system of work is.

What you should do for your site and employer

1. Understand what signs and signals mean.

2. Speak to your supervisor if you are confused by a sign or there seems to be too many signs.

3. Follow the instruction or direction on any sign or signal.

4. Do not vandalise or remove any sign.

5. Report any damaged or missing signs.

C 10

Mandatory signs (must do)

General mandatory

Safety harness must be worn

Safety helmet must be worn

Eye protection must be worn

Safety boots must be worn

Safety gloves must be worn

C
10

Prohibition signs (ban or disallow)

No pedestrians

No smoking

No escape route

Children must not play on this site

Scaffolding incomplete Do not use

Warning signs

General warning

Forklifts at work

Flammable

Explosive

Corrosive

Toxic

Danger of electrocution

Fragile roof

Radioactive

Laser beams

C
10

Confined space **No unauthorised entry**

 Danger Men working overhead

 Danger Falling objects

 Danger Asbestos removal in progress

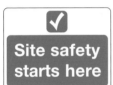 **Warning** Stand clear of suspended loads

 Caution Trip hazard

C
10

Emergency and first aid signs

 **Site safety starts here**

Assembly point

First aid

Wash your hands

Emergency eyewash

Emergency shower

Fire-fighting signs

Fire hose

Ladder

Emergency fire telephone

Fire extinguisher telephone

C
10

11

Fire prevention and control

What your site and employer should do for you

1. Put in place a fire prevention and fire action plan.

2. Explain the fire risks and controls.

3. Provide and maintain fire detection, fire-fighting equipment and fire exits.

4. Have a system to control 'hot work'.

5. Provide means to ensure rubbish and waste doesn't build up.

What you should do for your site and employer

1. Practise good housekeeping and clear up your waste.

2. Get a hot-work permit whenever you might create sparks, heat or flames.

3. Keep exit routes and fire points clear at all times.

4. Store materials and fuels in designated areas..

5. Know what to do and how to raise the alarm in the event of a fire.

C
11

Introduction

Fire kills about 750 people every year in the UK and injures many more. Depending upon the stage of construction or refurbishment, sites can be at a higher risk and fire and smoke can spread rapidly.

Fire

How fire starts

For fire to start there must be three elements (the fire triangle):

- [✓] heat or ignition (such as a spark)
- [✓] fuel (something flammable)
- [✓] oxygen (air).

Fighting fire

Fire-fighting equipment works by removing:

- [✓] heat (cooling with water)
- [✓] the fuel
- [✓] oxygen (smothering with foam or a fire blanket).

**C
11**

Hot works

Hot work can be any work where heat, sparks or naked flames are produced (such as welding, grinding or soldering).

A hot-work permit will tell you:

- [✓] when to start
- [✓] how to prevent hot sparks travelling
- [✓] what fire extinguisher you should have close by
- [✓] if you need a fire watch
- [✓] when you must stop
- [✓] when you must go back and recheck (one or two hours after hot work ends).

Fire-fighting equipment signs

Fire
point

Hose reel

Call point

Types of portable fire extinguisher

C
11

*Water
(red label)*

*Foam
(cream label)*

*Powder (all types)
(blue label)*

*Carbon dioxide
(black label)*

*Wet chemical
(yellow label)*

Using portable fire extinguishers

It is vital that everyone is vigilant and any hot work is controlled. The table on the following page shows the types of portable fire extinguishers and what to use them on.

Fire class	Substances, materials, and so on	Water (red label)	Foam (cream label)	Carbon dioxide (CO_2) (black label)	Dry powder (blue label)
A	Carbonaceous and organic materials, wood, paper, rag, textile, cardboard, common plastics, laminates, foam.	YES, excellent	YES	Difficult to use outdoors in windy conditions. For small fires only if no water available	YES
B	Flammable liquids, petrol, oil, fats, adhesives, paint, varnish.	NO	YES, if liquid is not flowing	YES, but not ideal	YES
C	Flammable gas: LPG, butane, propane, methane, acetylene.	NO, not effective on gas flame but will cool the area and put out secondary fires	YES, if in liquid form. (Seek specialist advice.)	NO	YES, excellent
D	Metal, molten metal, reactive metal powder.	NO	NO	NO	YES, trained person – if no explosive risk. Special powders are available, but DRY sand or earth may be used
E	Electrical installations, typewriters, VDUs, computers, photocopiers, televisions, and so on.	NO	NO	YES	YES, but not ideal. Or switch off electricity and deal with as an ordinary fire
F	Fires with cooking appliances that involve vegetable or animal fat.	NO	YES, with F rating only.	YES, with F rating only.	YES, with F rating only.

C
11

C
11

12

Electrical safety and hand-held tools and equipment

What your site and employer should do for you

1. Provide safe, temporary electrics and safety lighting.

2. Isolate and protect from existing main, underground and overhead supplies.

3. Provide the right tools, equipment and PPE for the job.

4. Provide information and training so you know how to use them safely.

5. Ensure electrical installations, tools and equipment are maintained.

What you should do for your site and employer

1. Use battery or 110 volt tools and equipment where possible.

2. Only use other voltages if part of a safe system of work.

3. Select, check and use the correct equipment and PPE.

4. Only use tools and equipment if you have the correct training.

5. Report any damage or faults.

C 12

Electricity – what's the problem?

You can't see it, you can't smell it, it's dangerous and it can kill.

☑ There is no visible way of knowing for sure if a cable or wires are live.

☑ If there are cables or wires near where you are working, assume they are live and report them.

☑ The temporary nature of site electrical distribution systems and the possibility of them being damaged are more reason to be careful with electricity.

Electrical voltages

Battery power

☑ Battery-powered tools are by far the safest option.

☑ They will not give you an electric shock.

☑ There are no trailing leads.

☑ A lot of sites now provide secure battery charging lockers.

110 volt – yellow

☑ Electrical tools should be 110 volt on construction sites.

☑ The standard colour code for 110 volt equipment is yellow.

☑ The 110 volt system means you would only get a 55 volt shock.

☑ You would feel it but no lasting damage should be done.

230 volt – blue

☑ The standard colour for 230 volt outdoor use is blue.

☑ It is commonly used for generators and electrical distribution.

☑ Domestic voltage or mains power is 230 volts.

☑ You will get a severe or even fatal electric shock if you touch a live 230 volt cable.

☑ This is why 230 volt tools are banned on most sites.

415 volt – red

☑ The standard colour for 415 volt is red.

☑ It is for equipment needing a lot of power (such as a tower crane).

**C
12**

Using extension leads and cables

☑ Always fully unwind an extension reel or cable.

☑ A part unwound cable can overheat, melt and catch fire.

☑ Where possible, route cables or leads overhead.

☑ Cables on the floor are trip hazards.

☑ Protect cables from being run over with protective ramps.

☑ Don't route cables across puddles or waterlogged ground.

☑ Get a transformer moved rather than using several leads joined together.

Electrical hazards

☑ There may be overhead power lines on site, which are only completely safe if switched off.

☑ People have been electrocuted and killed when items (such as ladders, towers or mobile plant) accidently touch or come close to them.

☑ If a 230 volt fuse blows, check equipment and leads for damage first.

☑ If you see smoke from a power tool, switch it off and take it out of use.

☑ Burn, scorch marks or burning odours indicate an electrical fault.

☑ Damaged leads and cables, even just the outer sheathing, must be taken out of use.

Protection devices

☑ You must use a residual current device (RCD) with any 230 volt tool and only after permission.

☑ RCDs work by cutting the power quickly if there is a fault.

☑ They fit between the plug and the socket.

☑ Check the RCD is working by pressing the test button before use.

Portable appliance testing

☑ Tools, leads and equipment should be tested every three months if used on site.

☑ The portable appliance testing (PAT) test label will tell you when the next safety check is due.

C 12

Hand-held tools and equipment – what's the problem?

Many types of power tools and hand tools are used in the construction industry. Thousands of injuries occur from the use of hand-held tools and equipment.

Moving parts, rotating blades and drill bits can cause serious injury in an instant. As can non-powered hand tools (such as handsaws, trimming knives and hammers).

Because they are used regularly you can become complacent to the hazards and risks.

 Noise and vibration from using hand-held equipment can pose a risk to health. Refer to Chapter B07 for further information.

Safe methods of working

Competence

To operate powered hand tools and equipment you must be competent. You need:

- ☑ training to be able to use certain tools
- ☑ knowledge of the tool and the hazards
- ☑ experience gained by using the tool
- ☑ an understanding of the environment the tool is to be used in and its limitations.

C
12

Before using any tool:

- ☑ check it's the right tool for the job
- ☑ carry out a pre-use visual check
- ☑ ensure it has been maintained.

Guards and safety features

- ☑ Always isolate the power when changing bits or adjusting guards on power tools.
- ☑ Ensure all guards or other safety features (such as emergency stops) are in place and work.
- ☑ Adjust the guard so you can see what you are doing and to minimise the gap between it and the moving part.
- ☑ Never carry out any makeshift repairs or modifications.

Protect yourself

- ☑ Most power tool noise levels mean you should be wearing hearing protection.
- ☑ Do not exceed daily safe vibration exposure times.
- ☑ Wear the correct eye protection.

☑ Avoid loose clothing and neck drawstrings and make sure the power lead doesn't get entangled in moving parts, which can cause serious injury.

☑ Keep hands from moving parts – gloved fingers which have a good grip can 'stick' to a drill chuck, wrenching your fingers around it instantly.

Types of hand-held equipment

Petrol-driven hand tools

☑ Petrol must be kept in small quantities in approved containers.

☑ Refuel only in well-ventilated areas using a funnel.

☑ Do not refuel with the engine running or while parts are still hot.

☑ Exhaust fumes are toxic and must not accumulate in enclosed or confined spaces.

Abrasive wheels and diamond blades

☑ Common machines include:
- petrol cut off saws (disc cutters)
- angle grinders
- tile cutters
- masonry bench saws
- wall chasers and floor saws.

☑ Abrasive wheels and diamond blades can burst, shatter or suffer high speed segment loss if not used correctly, resulting in horrific injuries.

☑ You must be trained and competent to change or mount a wheel or blade.

☑ The speed of the wheel or blade must match the machine speed.

☑ Only cut material the wheel or blade is made for.

☑ Diamond blades can fail in lots of different ways if misused.

☑ Diamond blade manufacturers supply free inspection and fault-finding guides.

☑ Eye protection (impact goggles) must be worn.

 Using a concrete diamond blade on tarmac can seriously weaken the blade. The result is that nail-sized segments can fly off at very high speeds.

C 12

Electrical hand tools

☑ All electrical hand tools used on site should only be 110 volt.

☑ Before every use you should carry out a brief visual inspection of:
   – power lead and plug
   – casing
   – switches, triggers and guards.

☑ You must switch off and remove the plug before carrying out any adjustment.

Cartridge-operated tools

☑ These work like a gun by firing an explosive charge.

☑ They are used to fire fixings into solid surfaces (such as concrete or steel columns).

☑ These are very dangerous in untrained hands.

☑ You must be trained to use a cartridge-operated tool.

☑ Tool manufacturers often offer free on-site training.

☑ Cartridge-operated tools need to be inspected, regularly cleaned and oiled.

☑ Eye protection (impact goggles) and hearing protection must be worn.

C
12

Compressed gas tools (nail guns)

☑ They need to be inspected, cleaned and oiled regularly.

☑ Eye protection (impact goggles) must be worn.

☑ Remove battery, fuel cell and remaining nails before clearing a blockage.

☑ Fuel cells or canisters must be disposed of correctly.

☑ Tool manufacturers often offer free on-site training.

Chainsaws

☑ Chainsaws can inflict horrific injuries.

☑ The main danger is they have a fully exposed cutting chain.

☑ Chainsaws can kick back, that is uncontrollably kick upwards towards the operator with the chain running.

☑ You must be fully trained, competent and wearing full chainsaw protective body clothing and head protection.

Compressed air-powered tools

☑ Compressed air tools are attached to a compressor using air hoses.

☑ Tools include heavy duty breakers, soil picks, concrete scabblers and pokers.

☑ Always check hose fittings are tight and secure before use.

☑ High pressure air hoses can cause serious injury if they break away from the compressor or tool. Whip checks should be used on every hose joint to prevent this.

Non-powered hand tools

☑ These may seem low risk, but are responsible for many injuries.

☑ They need to be well maintained and regularly inspected.

☑ Well used chisels and bolsters can form 'mushroom heads'. When they are struck fragments can fly into the air and into the eye.

☑ Loose handles, blunt blades and worn parts all pose a risk.

Lasers

☑ If used correctly lasers should not pose a health hazard.

☑ A rotating laser means it's difficult to look directly at the beam for more than an instant.

☑ Static lasers (such as pipe lasers), pose more of a risk.

☑ Exclusion zones and warning signs must be in place if high-powered lasers are being used.

C
12

13

Site transport safety

What your site and employer should do for you

1. Explain the site traffic rules to you at induction.

2. Provide signage, markings, barriers and lighting.

3. Separate routes for pedestrians and vehicles.

4. Provide safe methods for deliveries, unloading and parking.

5. Arrange one-way systems, speed limits and banned or controlled reversing.

What you should do for your site and employer

1. Follow all signs and speed limits.

2. Only use designated walking routes.

3. Liaise with the site manager first if you have to drive your vehicle on site.

4. Report any plant movement you think is unsafe or too close to your work.

5. Always wear your high-visibility clothing.

C
13

Introduction

The movement and operation of vehicles and plant causes many accidents and serious injuries on sites each year. The accidents involve not only the operator but persons working close by or just walking past.

Mobile plant and site vehicles

The term *mobile plant* will be used in this section to cover all mobile plant and site vehicles that can move either under their own power or by being towed, such as:

- ☑ dumpers
- ☑ excavators
- ☑ telehandlers and forklifts
- ☑ mobile cranes and piling rigs
- ☑ HGVs, lorries and delivery wagons
- ☑ vans and cars
- ☑ road rollers, including pedestrian-operated rollers.

The term *operator* will be used to describe anyone driving or operating mobile plant and *pedestrians* will be anyone on foot.

C
13

Accidents

The most common causes of accidents are:

- ☑ being struck by reversing or moving mobile plant
- ☑ loss of control, overturning when working, travelling across or manoeuvring on slopes
- ☑ people falling when climbing in and out of the machine
- ☑ accidental operation of mobile plant that has been left with the engine running – often caused as operators are getting in and out of the machine
- ☑ being crushed between a structure and mobile plant as it moves or slews around.

Many accidents involving mobile plant happen because plant is large and the operator has a restricted view. Extra mirrors and CCTV are sometimes fitted to improve the operator's all-round vision – but don't depend upon it.

If you are close to moving or operating mobile plant you could be at risk. Whenever possible, stay within the designated pedestrian routes.

A mobile crane slewing, an excavator digging or a lorry tipping material, whilst not actually travelling, can still be a danger if you get too close.

Never assume an operator will see you in time to avoid you.

At the very least, a signaller should be directing the operation or movement of plant in situations where other people could be at risk, (such as when a lorry is reversing or when a crane is carrying out a lift).

If you are the operator and you lose sight of the signaller, you must stop and locate them before continuing.

 Do not attempt to operate any item of plant if you are not competent and authorised.

At the very least, a signaller should be directing the operation or movement of plant in situations.

The chance of an accident between mobile plant and people on foot can increase after dark. Even when wearing high-visibility clothing, if the lighting is poor the operator may still not realise you are there. The use of working lights could improve safety.

 After dark and at other times when the light is not so good, remember that you will be more difficult to see.

C
13

Common types of accidents

The operator's field of vision is restricted

People have been seriously injured or killed when trying to pass too close to moving or reversing mobile plant.

Slewing plant

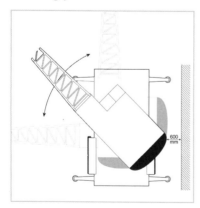

As the rear of a slewing crane or excavator turns, the gap between the rear of the machine and a fixed object (such as a wall, stack of materials or other plant) suddenly becomes much smaller (a crush zone).

☑ If the gap is 600 mm or less during slewing then the gap must be fenced or blocked off.

If you are operating plant (such as a pedestrian roller or MEWP), always be aware of what is behind or above – you may create your own crush zone.

This type of accident can happen because people on foot did not stay clear of mobile plant, took a short cut or followed a route that was not safe.

 Stay out of the crush zone. The shortest route may not be the safest route.

Management of mobile plant

A well-managed site will be organised to reduce the chance of accidents between mobile plant and people on foot. Measures will be taken such as:

- ☑ separate routes for mobile plant and people on foot with barriers between them
- ☑ separate site entrances for mobile plant and pedestrians
- ☑ one-way systems and site speed limits
- ☑ reversing banned or minimised by the use of turning areas
- ☑ amber flashing beacons on mobile plant
- ☑ a signaller to control movement of mobile plant
- ☑ ensuring all lights are working and on during poor light levels and after dark.

Whether you are an operator or not, the site rules on the safe operation and segregation of mobile plant should be explained to you during your site induction.

Your actions can make a difference

C
13

- ☑ If you cannot avoid passing close to mobile plant, or you need to speak to the operator, you will have to be patient and wait in a safe place until:
  - – it has finished the job and stopped moving or working
  - – it has moved away altogether
  - – the operator knows that you are there, the plant stops operating and you are signalled to go past.

- ☑ Stay out of plant compounds and other parking areas unless your work takes you there, in which case be alert to plant starting up and moving off, and keep out of its way.

- ☑ Do not ask for or accept rides on plant that is not designed to carry passengers. Deaths have been caused by unauthorised passengers clinging onto an item of plant then losing their grip and falling under the wheels or tracks.

- ☑ Always wear your high-visibility clothing and keep it reasonably clean.

☑ Report to your supervisor or employer any aspect of plant operations that you think is a danger. For example, where mobile plant:

- is operating too close for comfort
- travels or operates too fast and is a danger to other people
- ignores one-way systems
- uses routes that are only intended for pedestrians
- looks to be defective.

Sometimes there isn't time to tell your supervisor or employer about a problem. If it's safe to do so then warn the operator and maybe others in the area.

Hand signals for slingers

Knowing these signals will help you be aware of the dangers. However, you must not signal to plant operators unless you have been trained to do so.

Start

Stop

Danger: emergency stop

Left

C
13

Right

Raise

Lower

Move backwards

Move forwards

Jib up

Jib down

Extend jib

C
13

Retract jib

End

C
13

14

Working at height

What your site and employer should do for you

1. Ensure work at height is planned, so proper precautions are put in place.

2. Provide systems to:

    – prevent you falling (such as mobile tower)

    – collect you or stop you if you fall (such as harness).

3. Provide the correct work at height equipment and ensure it is inspected and maintained.

4. Give you information and instruction so you can work at height safely.

What you should do for your site and employer

1. Follow the agreed safe system of work.

2. Use only equipment and methods you have been trained in.

3. Not misuse any equipment.

4. Not take risks or short cuts.

5. Stop and seek advice if anything changes or seems unsafe.

D
14

Introduction

☑ Falls continue to be the biggest cause of fatal injury in Britain's workplaces.

☑ On average there are 50 fatalities a year in construction – around half are falls from height.

☑ 60% of all work at height injuries are from falls below head height.

☑ Most falls were caused by not using the right piece of equipment for the job.

 What can you fall from?

Many falls were from ladders, stepladders or improvised platforms, which offer little or no fall protection.

Falls through fragile roofs, skylights and openings still happen far too frequently.

For all work at height, measures must be taken to prevent the risk of any fall that could cause injury as there is no distinction made between low and high falls.

Work at height is work at **any** height where a person could fall and be injured. It also includes instances (such as working next to an open excavation) because of the risk of falling in.

What your employer should do

☑ Identify jobs that involve work at height.

☑ Plan the work to ensure that appropriate precautions are in place.

☑ Select and use the right equipment.

☑ Make sure that people working at height are competent.

☑ Communicate risk control measures to the workforce.

☑ Ensure the equipment is regularly inspected and maintained.

D
14

Planning the work

☑ A risk assessment must be undertaken for all work at height.

☑ It should take into account things such as:
  - the complexity of the work being done
  - who is doing the work and for how long
  - weather conditions and surface conditions (such as wet sloping roof)
  - how to raise and store materials and equipment.

 When anyone is planning work at height they must follow the hierarchy of control measures.

You should also follow the hierarchy when selecting any access equipment.

Hierarchy for working at height

Step 1. Avoid working at height
e.g. assemble on the ground and crane up, use extendable handles on equipment.

Only if this can't be avoided then:

Step 2. Use an existing safe place of work
e.g. parapet walls, defined access points, staircases.

Only if this can't be done then:

Step 3. Provide work equipment to prevent falls
e.g. scaffolding, edge protection, handrails, podiums, mobile towers, MEWPs.

Only if this can't be provided then:

Step 4. Mitigate distance and consequence of a fall
e.g. safety netting, airbags, crash decks
(harnesses must be used as a last resort).

Step 5. Provide instruction, training and/or other means
e.g. PASMA training for mobile towers, IPAF training for MEWPs,
using ladders (the **last resort**).

Working at height

- ☑ Safe access (such as a tower staircase or tied ladder) must be provided.
- ☑ Edge protection (such as temporary guard-rails) must be put in place.
- ☑ Barriers should be set back from the edge.
- ☑ Surfaces can become very slippery when wet or frosty.
- ☑ You should not work on any structure where there is no protection from falls.
- ☑ If you are working on a leading edge then measures (such as safety nets) should be installed. Harnesses may only be used as a last resort.

D
14

Fragile roofs

Sadly there are many fatal and serious injuries from people falling through fragile roofs and roof lights.

Asbestos cement sheets are obvious, but fragile roof lights, which look like the more secure surrounding roof structure over time, are not so obvious. Other materials include glass, plastics and old, unstable structures.

Many people are not aware that parts of a roof are fragile. Others may think that the roof will take their weight or they will try to walk near the underlying supports. Be aware that it may be difficult to see a fragile surface, especially if the roof is dirty, covered by moss or if it has been painted.

Use crawling boards

Safety signs to BS 5378

DANGER
Fragile roof

If work on a roof cannot be avoided a safe system of work **must** be put in place by:

- ☑ providing a suitable access (such as a stair tower or ladder) or accessing the area with a MEWP
- ☑ providing stagings with handrails, which are sufficient to span the underlying supports
- ☑ installing safety netting, crash decks or airbags underneath the roof.

If this is not possible then crawling boards to spread the weight should be provided.

Where harnesses are in use an anchorage point must be provided and be properly used.

D
14

 Never attempt to access or cross a fragile roof light without a safe access system.

Voids and holes

Any hole or void where a person could fall any distance and hurt themselves must be protected. These include:

- ☑ floor and roof openings
- ☑ floor joists and roof trusses
- ☑ lift shaft openings
- ☑ service holes and risers
- ☑ open manholes and other voids.

Any opening must be protected with secure barriers, covers, gates or doors, which are secured in position and display appropriate warning signs.

☑ Never remove a protective cover unless authorised to do so.

☑ If you think something should be covered speak to your supervisor, employer or site manager.

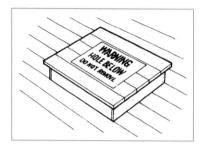 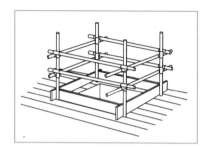

Preventing falls

The best prevention of falls of persons should be by physical barriers and equipment.

☑ Methods include: Scaffolding, mobile towers, mobile elevating work platforms (MEWPs), podiums, edge protection systems.

☑ The minimum height of any guard-rail is 950 mm.

☑ Any gap on the barrier must be not more than 470 mm.

☑ Plastic barriers, netting or rope and pins are not suitable as edge protection to prevent persons from falling.

Netting, brick guards or solid boards should be used to prevent falls of materials.

If a guard-rail has to be moved, it must only be done with permission and only by a trained and competent person. The guard-rail must be replaced as soon as possible.

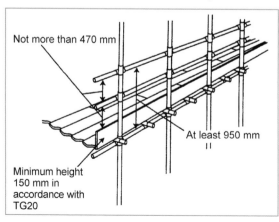

Not more than 470 mm

At least 950 mm

Minimum height 150 mm in accordance with TG20

D
14

Arresting falls

☑ If falls can't be prevented then the risk of injury must be minimised.

☑ Fall-arrest systems include air/bean bags, safety netting and crash decks.

☑ The safe system of work must contain a system for emergency rescue.

Harnesses

Harnesses should only be used if falls can't be prevented by physical barriers or minimised by using fall collection systems.

☑ Harnesses are there to protect a person if they fall.

☑ The selection of the type of harness and lanyard to be used is vital. It should take into account where it is being used, how far the wearer may fall, any obstructions they may hit and any pendulum effect.

☑ You must receive training before using a harness and lanyard.

☑ It is vital you know how to inspect a harness for damage, how to fit it properly, where to attach it and where not to attach it.

A harness could be the one thing preventing you falling to your death.

 Never use a harness to work at height unless you have been trained.

There must be an effective rescue plan in place in case a person wearing a harness falls as:

☑ they need to be reached very quickly

☑ when someone is arrested and suspended in a harness their body can suffer from complications (this is known as suspension trauma)

☑ people who have fallen wearing a harness could die from suspension trauma after they have been rescued.

D 14

Types of access equipment

Mobile elevating work platforms

☑ Common types are scissor lifts and cherry pickers.

☑ You must only use these if you have been fully trained and are competent.

☑ If you are a passenger in a cherry picker type MEWP you must wear a full body harness and lanyard clipped to the designed attachment point in the basket.

☑ **Never** clip onto an adjacent structure.

Scaffolding

☑ Scaffolding must only be erected, altered or dismantled by trained and competent scaffolders.

☑ Any platform you are working on must have guard-rails and toe-boards fitted.

☑ Keep the scaffold working platform clean and tidy.

☑ MEWPs should not be used for accessing scaffolds or other structures.

☑ Brick-guards must be fitted if materials are stored above toe-board height.

Do not access scaffolding if you see this sign.

Scaffolding
incomplete
Do not use

Mobile tower scaffolds

Mobile towers are safe and versatile access equipment if used correctly. Unfortunately, many towers are not erected or used correctly and are the cause of numerous accidents each year.

You must hold a PASMA or equivalent qualification to erect, alter or dismantle a mobile tower.

If you are only working on a tower, as a minimum you should receive a toolbox talk on the risks and hazards associated with using towers.

It should cover common risks such as:

☑ locking wheel brakes

☑ using only the internal ladder to access the deck

☑ checking that guard-rails and toe-boards are fitted (these must not be removed)

☑ making sure that:

  – working platforms are not fitted too high so that guard-rails are too low

  – towers are not overloaded

  – the hatch is closed when working on the platform.

D
14

Podiums

Podiums have become very popular pieces of access equipment. They:

☑ are safe and versatile access equipment if used correctly

☑ can be unstable and topple over if not assembled or used correctly.

Stepladders

There is a wide variety of stepladders on the market. Some offer very good fall protection and others less so.

Platform step

They should only be considered for light work of short duration and where the use of other, more suitable work equipment is not appropriate.

Wherever possible, platform steps should be the preferred option over traditional swing-back steps.

Stepladders should be used only when it's not possible to use other access methods.

☑ Always check they are in good condition before use.

☑ Always use on firm, level ground.

☑ Always make sure they are fully extended and face forward towards the steps.

☒ Never over reach.

☒ Never stand on the top four treads or top third of any stepladder unless it is designed to be used this way.

D 14

Ladders

☑ These are the most commonly used pieces of access equipment for a wide range of tasks.

☑ They are also the most misused when used as a working platform.

☑ It is essential that those who use ladders are trained and competent to do so.

☑ Ladders should be your **last option.**

☑ They should only be considered for light work of short duration and where the use of other, more suitable work equipment is not appropriate.

☑ Always check a ladder before use.

☑ A painted ladder can hide defects or damaged parts.

☑ Report any defects to your supervisor.

☒ Ladders or stepladders should not be used 6 m horizontally of any power lines, unless the line has been made dead.

If ladders are used, they should:

- ☑ be of the correct type – Class 1 industrial or EN131
- ☑ be in good condition
- ☑ be placed on firm and level ground
- ☑ be properly secured (tied at the top)
- ☑ use outriggers if available
- ☑ be set at the correct length and angle for the job – 75° or a ratio of 1:4 (one out to four up)
- ☑ extend one metre or five rungs past the stepping off point.

You should have three points of contact at all times.

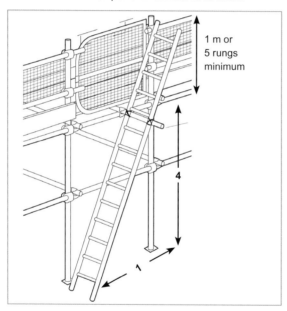

1 m or
5 rungs
minimum

4

1

15

Excavations and confined spaces

What your site and employer should do for you

1. Make sure that you do not have to enter an excavation unless the sides have adequate support to prevent collapse.

2. Prevent persons, materials and vehicles from falling into excavations.

3. If your job involves or creates a confined space, ensure this has been identified.

4. Assess the risks and develop a safe system of work.

5. Only allow persons who are confined space trained under a permit.

What you should do for your site and employer

1. Do not enter any excavation which is unsupported.

2. Install supports following the safe system of work.

3. Do not leave any open excavation unguarded.

4. Do not enter a confined space unless a safe system of work is in place and you are trained to do so.

5. Do not take any risks.

D
15

Excavations – what's the problem?

Generally speaking, an excavation is any hole or trench dug into the ground as part of construction or utility work. Some excavations are knee deep, but many are deeper. They do not need to be deep before becoming a serious risk or a confined space.

Every year deaths and injuries occur due to collapsing excavations, workers being overcome by poisonous gases or striking live services.

Collapse

Excavations and trenches collapse because:

- ☑ the sides are not supported or supports are not installed properly

- ☑ vehicles operate too close to the edge (for example dumpers, excavators, concrete wagons)

- ☑ materials and spoil are stored too close to the edge

- ☑ the ground dries out, shrinks and collapses

- ☑ heavy rain weakens the ground and the sides

- ☑ the excavation undermines or weakens nearby walls and structures, which causes collapse.

 Excavations are dangerous

A cubic metre of soil can weigh over a tonne (1,000 kg).

A shallow excavation can easily collapse onto you if you are bending over.

It can easily crush your legs, hips or chest and prevent you breathing.

Collapse is silent and without warning.

D 15

Safe systems of work to follow include:

- ☑ avoiding the need for anyone to go into an excavation

- ☑ installing excavation supports before anyone goes into an excavation

- ☑ using methods that protect the person installing the support system

- ☑ only working within the safety of the protected area on long open excavations (for example within the sides of a 'drag box' or trench supports)

- ☑ providing a safe way to get in and out (such as a tied ladder)

- ☑ providing fall prevention around the excavation (such as a handrail or extended trench sheets)

- ☑ preventing vehicles from coming too close (for example using wheel stop blocks).

A visual inspection must be carried out before each shift.

A written weekly inspection must be carried out if the excavation is open more than seven days.

Keep vehicles a safe distance away from the edge of an excavation. A full 6 m³ concrete wagon weighs 26 tonnes.

Poisonous or flammable gases and fumes

Poisonous gases and fumes can be heavier than air and can 'pour' over the edges and start filling up an excavation or a confined space. These can include:

- [✓] exhaust fumes from petrol or diesel-powered plant
- [✓] naturally occurring gases (such as methane), which seep out of the ground
- [✓] fumes from solvents (such as welding plastic pipes, epoxy resins or sealants)
- [✓] liquefied petroleum gas (LPG) or pipe freezing sprays.

Safe systems of work may include:

- [✓] continuous monitoring of the air using a gas detector
- [✓] pumping in fresh air
- [✓] regularly stirring up the atmosphere with a digger bucket
- [✓] using a solvent free product that does not give off fumes
- [✓] wearing breathing apparatus.

 Always be aware of gas hazards

You may not be able to see or smell gas in an excavation.

If you are in an excavation and feel light headed, dizzy or can smell gas:

Warn others – get out – stay out – report it immediately.

D
15

Buried services

- [✓] Electricity cables.
- [✓] Gas mains.
- [✓] Water mains.
- [✓] Sewers and drains.
- [✓] Telecommunications, fibre optics.
- [✓] Oil or fuel pipes.

Thousands of service strikes happen every year. Many result in injury and some are fatal. It is vital that any excavation, no matter how big or small, deep or shallow is properly planned.

Before digging, every effort should be made to locate existing services. These methods will **indicate** approximately where the services are.

- [✓] Refer to existing service drawings.
- [✓] Phone up the utility company.

☑ Carry out a ground radar survey.

☑ Use cable avoidance tool detection (such as CAT and Genny equipment).

Hand digging trial holes to expose the services is the most accurate way of locating them.

Safe systems of work may include:

☑ do not use forks near live buried services

☑ always treat services as live unless confirmed otherwise

☑ never assume a service runs in a straight line

☑ some services have marker tape or tiles laid above them to warn of their presence

☑ if you find an unexpected buried service, report it immediately

☑ if you strike a live service – get out quickly, warn others and report it.

Confined spaces – what's the problem?

Workers can become trapped or overcome by fumes, vapours, explosive or poisonous gases when working in confined spaces. In many cases this can lead to the person dying.

Many workers who attempted to rescue workmates without a proper rescue plan have been overcome by the gas and fumes themselves and also collapsed and died, adding to the tragedy.

What is a confined space?

Confined spaces are not just tanks or chambers. They do not have to be totally enclosed.

**D
15**

They can be any area where there is a risk of:

☑ reduced oxygen in the air

☑ the presence of poisonous gases or fumes

☑ the presence of flammable or explosive gases or vapours.

Depending upon the work hazards many areas could be classed as a confined space. Examples are:

☑ excavations, trenches

☑ manholes, inspection chambers, sewers, soakaways

☑ service tunnels, plant rooms, boiler rooms

☑ basements, voids, staircases

☑ lofts, attics

☑ unventilated rooms, rooms with windows and doors closed

☑ oil storage tanks or water tanks above ground.

An unventilated room may not seem like a confined space. However, if you are using a substance in the room that gives off hazardous vapours then you could become unconscious.

The hazards

Reduced oxygen levels

Oxygen, which we need to breathe, can be reduced by:

- ☑ hot works or jobs that burn up the oxygen
- ☑ people breathing
- ☑ rust inside enclosed tanks.

Build up of poisonous or flammable gases

Oxygen levels can be replaced by poisonous or flammable gases by:

- ☑ stirring up sludge or slurry in excavations
- ☑ natural methane from the ground or rotting vegetation
- ☑ using substances that give off fumes or vapours
- ☑ sewage giving off hydrogen sulphide (smells like rotting eggs)
- ☑ chalky ground, which gives off carbon dioxide
- ☑ people breathing out carbon dioxide
- ☑ gases (such as LPG, methane or oxygen enrichment) which build up to form a highly flammable atmosphere.

An overturned tanker or a large spill may release petrol or dangerous chemicals into the drainage system. The vapours can travel hundreds of metres.

Working in a confined space

Your employer should identify if the work activity hazards and area of work mean it is classed as a confined space. Anyone working in a confined space must be trained.

Work in a confined space needs three safety documents to form a safe system of work:

- ☑ method statement
- ☑ risk assessment
- ☑ permit to work (this manages entry and control).

D
15

The safe system of work will identify key issues:

☑ who can enter and for how long (time limits)

☑ how to get in and out safely

☑ what tools and materials to use and how

☑ what personal protective equipment to use

☑ the type of air monitoring equipment and alarm system

☑ the emergency arrangements

☑ the rescue equipment and trained rescue personnel.

The air must be constantly monitored before and during entry using a meter with an alarm. Usually there is one person (called the 'topman') at the entrance to the confined space whose job is to get the rescue plan underway if things go wrong.

 Never attempt to rescue someone unless you are part of a trained rescue team. Use the time to get expert help or call the emergency services.

D
15

Excavations and confined spaces

16

Environmental awareness and waste control

What your site and employer should do for you

1.	Explain any specific environmental issues at site induction.
2.	Develop and let you know methods to avoid pollution.
3.	Provide means to distribute, store and use materials to avoid damage.
4.	Provide means to dispose of waste correctly.
5.	Provide emergency response methods (such as spill kits).

What you should do for your site and employer

1.	Reuse materials where possible.
2.	Dispose of waste correctly.
3.	Avoid creating excessive dust or noise.
4.	Turn off plant, equipment and taps when not in use.
5.	Know where the spill kit is, how to use it and report any incidents.

E
16

Sustainability

You will increasingly hear the word 'sustainability' being used in connection with construction work. The drive to carry out construction in a sustainable manner affects everyone in and around the industry.

One element of sustainability is to carry out construction work in a responsible manner and to minimise environmental damage, which could otherwise cause problems for future generations.

Examples of good practice are:

☑ using locally produced materials and minimising transportation of raw materials and finished goods

☑ looking after the people who carry out construction work and using local labour and services to support the local economy

☑ saving energy wherever possible by turning off equipment when not in use

☑ not damaging the environment by causing pollution

☑ designing out waste

☑ using reclaimed materials or materials with a high recycled content

☑ reusing left over materials wherever possible to conserve raw materials and save the energy it would take to produce new

☑ segregating waste into different types so that it may be reused or recycled more easily.

 Water, energy, fuel, construction materials and time are often wasted on construction sites, practices which need to be stopped or at least reduced.

Pollution

What are the causes of pollution?

☑ Deliberately or accidentally allowing substances (such as cement, silt, grout, sewage, chemicals, oils/greases or vehicle fuels) to soak into the ground or contaminate rivers, streams and ditches.

☑ Allowing smoke, fumes or dust to contaminate the air.

☑ Causing excessive noise, light or vibration, which can affect the quality of life of people who live or work nearby.

☑ Not segregating contaminated materials from other waste (for example putting rags used to clean up an oil spillage in with general waste materials).

☑ The destruction or disturbance of the habitats of protected or invasive plants and species of wildlife.

E
16

Why does pollution occur?

☑ Substances entering rivers, streams, ditches, drains or the ground because they aren't stored correctly.

☑ Not having the equipment or a plan to control accidental spillages.

☑ Rain and muddy surface water running off site onto roads, into drains and watercourses.

☑ Not having properly protected storage areas, to contain the leaks or spills of harmful liquids (such as oils, fuels and solvents).

☑ The illegal burning of waste materials and fly tipping.

☑ The accumulation of hazardous substances and waste materials in unprotected areas, enabling them to be washed into the ground by rainwater.

☑ Failing to adequately protect waste material skips, resulting in rainwater washing harmful residues out.

☑ The poor planning, or lack of supervision, of work activities which can allow inappropriate actions or affect the quality of life of other people.

The responsibilities of the person in charge of the site

The person in change of the site has legal responsibilities to:

☑ prevent environmental damage during construction

☑ ensure harmful substances, including fuels, are stored and handled correctly to prevent spillage or pollution

☑ produce and keep up to date a site waste management plan (in England)

☑ ensure that materials are properly segregated into different types of waste

☑ use only registered waste carriers

☑ check waste is properly disposed of through licensed contractors and facilities

☑ keep correct records and documentation for all waste.

They should also work out ways of reusing or recycling as much waste material as is practical in line with industry commitments to reduce waste to landfill.

Your part in preventing environmental damage

You should be given instructions and advice during and after site induction so you understand:

☑ the environmental site rules (such as how to dispose of your waste)

☑ what damage your work can have on the surrounding environment

☑ what work controls are expected to avoid damage

☑ what you need to do as an individual

☑ what to do in an emergency.

E
16

Environmentally damaging substances

To avoid creating pollution you should always:

☑ follow the instructions in the COSHH assessment and any site rules when using any substance, particularly with regard to storage and disposal

☑ keep the lids on tins of paints, adhesives and solvents when not in use

☑ prevent spillages, particularly into open ground, by careful handling and decanting of harmful liquids

☑ keep harmful substances 10 m away from watercourses, drains, and so on

☑ minimise waste materials by storing anything that can be rain-damaged under cover.

 Pollution spreads easily

Spilt or leaking oils, including fuel, can be particularly damaging to the environment.

It is possible for spilt or leaking substances to soak deep into the ground and pollute groundwater, which in some cases becomes domestic drinking water.

5 litres of oil can contaminate an area **the size of two football pitches.**

If it gets into the **groundwater,** pollution may appear **several miles away.**

 Spilt materials must be properly contained using absorbent materials, not washed down with detergent.

When refuelling site vehicles or construction plant, this must be carried out in an area with a hard surface that prevents spilt fuel from soaking into the ground. If refuelling has to be carried out away from these areas, where the ground is unprotected:

☑ a drip tray must be used (this must be cleaned of any spilt fuel afterwards by using absorbent spill clean-up materials)

☑ refuelling must take place at least 10 m from watercourses or drains. (Where 10 m cannot be achieved speak with your supervisor who should then implement control measures.)

Regulatory bodies recommend that refuelling is always carried out under supervision.

Where possible, refuelling should be carried out using a pumped system through a nozzle fitted with an automatic cut-off to prevent over-filling and therefore spillages. Where necessary, funnels should be used to assist in preventing spills.

Do not dispose of harmful substances into drains or gullies. Site drain covers should be colour coded to indicate what is allowed to pass through the drain.

☑ Blue: surface water (such as clean, uncontaminated rainwater).

☑ Red: foul water (such as sewage and silty run-off water).

☑ Red 'C':   combined surface and foul water.

E 16

If the product you are using displays either of these signs on the label or COSHH assessment then it is harmful to the environment. Anything left over, including the container, must be disposed of in accordance with the label or site rules.

Environmentally damaging substances already in the ground

Ground that was used or built on before may contain hazardous substances. You must immediately **stop** and tell your supervisor if you find:

☑ soil that has a strange smell and/or appears to be oily

☑ fragments or clumps of fibres that could be asbestos or other hazardous materials.

If you become involved in pumping water out of an excavation (de-watering) you must be aware that 'silty water' must be treated before it can be discharged into surface water drains or ditches. Site management or your supervisor must make the decision upon whether the water is silty.

Nuisance

No-one on site, or off it, should have to suffer nuisance and possibly ill health, because of site activities.

If you think that your work might be a nuisance to other people you should report it to your supervisor, for example:

☑ causing excessive noise, particularly during unsocial hours

☑ creating vibration that can be felt off site

☑ generating smoke

☑ vehicle fumes being a nuisance to nearby properties or people

☑ creating off-site dust clouds from haul roads

☑ site lighting or task lights shining onto nearby properties or people, including road traffic

☑ mud or dust being deposited on public roads or footpaths.

E
16

Pollution incidents

If you are aware that an environmental incident or spill has occurred then act quickly and follow these simple steps: stop – contain – notify.

☑ **Stop** work immediately and prevent any more substance spilling (such as right an oil drum, close a valve).

☑ **Eliminate** any sources of ignition (such as switch off plant).

☑ **Assess** the situation. Ensure you have appropriate personal protective equipment (PPE) and wait for further assistance if this is required. Do not put yourself at risk.

☑ **Contain** the spill by building earth or sand bunds immediately.

☑ **Check** the spill has not reached any nearby drains, manholes, watercourses, ditches, ponds or other sensitive areas.

☑ **Bund** drains/manholes to stop the substance entering the drainage system.

☑ **Notify** your supervisor or employer of an incident as soon as possible.

☑ **Dispose** of all contaminated materials (such as absorbent granules, soil, cleaning cloths) used to contain a spill in the appropriate hazardous waste skip.

Report the facts to your supervisor or employer, who should notify, by the emergency hotline, the Environment Agency (in England): 0800 80 70 60 or Natural Resources Wales (in Wales): 0300 065 3000.

Waste materials

The construction industry produces over 75 million tonnes of waste each year, more than any other industry in the UK. Environmental damage can result from waste materials if:

☑ it is allowed to accumulate and is not protected from the weather and scavenging animals

☑ hazardous waste is mixed with other waste (such as asbestos cement mixed with rubble)

☑ it is illegally disposed of or fly-tipped.

E
16

Everyone on site has a part to play in preventing environmental damage by being aware of the potential environmental risks that arise from their work.

You have a responsibility for identifying how and where you create waste so that efforts can be made to reduce the amount produced. Always check if someone else can use what you are about to throw away as it might have a use elsewhere.

Different types of waste should be segregated into different skips so that it can be recycled more easily. Recycling waste means that it does not have to go to landfill.

To assist, colour coded labels are put on skips to indicate what type of waste should be put in them.

Label colour	Waste
Blue	Metallic
Green	Wood and timber
White	Plaster
Orange	Hazardous

 Hazardous waste must never be mixed in with other types of waste.

If it gets into landfill, hazardous waste can be very damaging to the environment.

Examples of hazardous waste

☑ Asbestos.

☑ Batteries.

☑ Used spill kits.

☑ Fluorescent light tubes.

☑ Waste solvents (such as white spirit, oil and bitumen based paints).

☑ Epoxy resins and mastics.

E
16

17

Demolition

What your site and employer should do for you

1. Provide you with a written method of working that is safe and without risks to your health (demolition plan).

2. Ensure that a competent person supervises the work, where necessary.

3. Inform you of the significant hazards identified in the risk assessment.

4. The safe way of working will be in a method statement which will be explained to you.

5. At no time place you in danger.

6. Provide you with adequate instruction and training.

What you should do for your site and employer

1. Follow the agreed safe system of work.

2. Not take risks with your or anyone else's health or safety.

3. Report any aspect of your work which you feel is unsafe or a threat to health.

4. Comply with any permit systems which are in operation.

F
17

Introduction

Demolition is a highly specialised and potentially dangerous activity. Health and safety law requires that it is only carried out by trained and competent demolition contractors.

☑ A competent person must be appointed to supervise the work before it starts.

☑ Prior to starting any demolition project, the risk assessment must be inspected to identify the intended way of controlling the hazards.

☑ If necessary a structural engineer must be consulted where it is thought that any part of the structure might collapse prematurely.

Planning the work

The demolition contractor must ensure that the work is planned and carried out in such a manner as to avoid danger, or where this is not possible, reduce the danger as far as is reasonably practicable. This will include:

☑ recording the arrangements for health and safety in writing before the work starts

☑ identifying, locating and isolating all services

☑ identifying the location of any asbestos through a demolition and refurbishment survey carried out before work starts, by a trained and competent asbestos surveyor

☑ identifying any other hazardous materials/substances and planning their removal

☑ laying out the sequence of operations in a written demolition plan and ensuring that it is read out during site induction and understood by all involved.

Safe methods of working

Given the potentially hazardous nature of demolition work, it is essential that safe methods of work are developed and followed.

☑ If demolishing internal brick walls, the operative must work across in even courses, from the ceiling down.

☑ The electricity company must be consulted if work has to be carried out near to overhead cables.

☑ If underground services that were not previously identified are discovered, work must stop until the situation has been resolved.

☑ When hinge-cutting a steel structure for a controlled collapse, the back-row bottom cuts must be made **last**.

☑ A gas-free certificate must be obtained before carrying out the demolition cutting of any fuel tank.

☑ Gas free certificates are only valid for 24 hours after being issued.

☑ Ensure the site is secure to prevent unauthorised access, particularly by children outside of working hours. (2.4 m hoardings or fencing is recommended.)

F
17

☑ Ensure there is sufficient clear signage (for example indicating the boundary of exclusion zones).

☑ Work at height must be carefully planned and carried out to prevent the fall of persons or materials.

☑ Do not allow combustible waste materials (demolition arisings) to accumulate.

Health hazards

Due to the nature of the working environment demolition can present some potentially serious, long-term threats to the health of the people involved if the risks are not controlled. Health issues are often overlooked because of the long-term nature of some diseases.

☑ Where asbestos is found to be present it must be removed, as far as is reasonably practicable, before the job starts.

☑ If during demolition it is suspected that some lead remains in the structure, work must stop immediately and a supervisor informed.

☑ Lead-based paint might be present under asbestos clad or coated steelwork.

☑ Anyone who has been exposed to lead must wash their hands and face before eating or drinking.

☑ Anyone involved in the hot cutting of coated steel must be aware of the potential for exposure to harmful levels of lead in the blood.

☑ COSHH assessments must cover any other harmful substances likely to be released.

☑ The safe system of work must prevent exposure to hand-arm vibration through the use of equipment (such as breakers or drills).

☑ Exposure to excessive hand-arm vibration can lead to vibration white finger.

☑ Demolition is likely to release airborne silica and other harmful dusts; the need for respiratory protective equipment (RPE) is covered later in this section.

☑ Skin diseases (such as dermatitis) must be prevented by ensuring there is no skin contact with harmful substances.

F
17

Personal protective equipment

Wearing the correct personal protective equipment (PPE) can prevent exposure to harmful substance; the wrong type of PPE is likely to be useless. The person in charge of the site must make sure that where necessary the correct PPE is worn, for example:

☑ higher grade RPE than might be necessary for work (FFP2 or FFP3, depending upon the protection factor required)

☑ a positive pressure-powered respirator, a compressed airline breathing apparatus or self-contained breathing apparatus is required if working in a dusty atmosphere.

   Note: a half-mask dust respirator does not provide the required level of protection

☑ a positive pressure-powered respirator or a ventilated respirator is provided when cutting coated steelwork.

Plant and equipment

Anyone who is required to operate any item of plant or equipment (for example a scissor lift) must be trained, competent and authorised.

☑ Information on the daily checks for mobile plant can be found:
   − on stickers attached to the machine
   − in the manufacturer's handbook
   − in additional information provided by the supplier of the machine.

☑ The extent of the daily checks that must be carried out by the operator include checking the emergency systems and the engine oil and hydraulic fluid levels.

☑ Operators must never attempt to move a machine if they do not have adequate visibility from the driving position (such as losing sight of the signaller).

☑ Unattended mobile plant must be left in a safe place with the keys removed and the doors locked.

☑ The head and tail lights of any machine must be switched on when the plant is operating in all conditions of poor visibility.

☑ An item of plant that has defective brakes must be isolated so that no-one else can try to use it and its condition must be reported.

☑ Machines that operate in areas where there may be falling materials must be fitted with a falling-object-protection system (FOPS).

☑ Roll-over protection (ROPS) must be fitted to plant to protect the driver where there is a danger of it rolling over.

☑ Operators must face the machine when climbing down from it.

☑ Passengers must only be carried on construction plant if a purpose-made passenger seat is fitted.

☑ All plant must be inspected, with the details recorded, at least every week.

F
17

☑ Plant movements and traffic routes must be planned and co-ordinated to ensure:
  - there is no conflict between different types of vehicles
  - the safety of pedestrians
  - the safe movement of materials
  - safe access to and egress from the site.

Lifting operations

Poorly thought out lifting operations and defective equipment have been the cause of many accidents.

☑ A method statement (lifting plan) must be drawn up for all lifting operations.

☑ Anyone not involved in lifting operations should be kept out of the area.

☑ Lifting equipment that is **not** used for lifting people must be thoroughly examined at least every 12 months.

☑ Lifting accessories (such as chains, shackles, slings, strops) and equipment used for lifting people must be thoroughly examined every six months.

☑ If any lifting accessory is found to be defective it must not be used and it must be isolated so that no-one can attempt to use it.

☑ All lifting operations must be carried out within the safe working load (SWL) of any item of lifting equipment and any lifting accessories used.

☑ The SWL must be marked upon each item of lifting equipment and each lifting accessory.

Confined spaces

Working in confined spaces is well know as a potentially hazardous activity. Many people have died through lack of planning or trying to rescue others.

☑ Before anyone starts working in a confined space they would be expected to refer to the risk assessment.

☑ During confined space working it is essential that the people doing the work strictly follow the conditions specified in the permit to work.

☑ Before entering any open-topped tank a permit to work must be obtained.

☑ Due to the fact that they contain a gas which is not breathable by human beings, no carbon dioxide extinguisher must ever be taken into a confined space.

LPG, other gases and substances

By the very nature of demolition activities, it is most likely that highly flammable and explosive substances will be stored and used on site at some time.

☑ It is essential that some gases are stored a safe distance away from other gases, (for example oxygen cylinders must be stored more than 3 m away from LPG cylinders).

☑ LPG cylinders that are used for heating or cooking in a site cabin must be stored outside the cabin.

☑ The correct type of fire extinguishers must be available where petrol or diesel are being stored, water extinguishers must **not** be provided.

☑ Flashback arrestors must be fitted between the pipes and gauges when using oxy-propane cutting equipment.

☑ Cans or drums of fluids must be stored in bunded areas to prevent any leaks from spreading.

☑ If unlabelled drums or containers are discovered, work must stop until they have been safely dealt with.

F
17

Demolition

18

Plumbing or gas

What your site and employer should do for you

1. Provide you with a method of working that is safe and without risks to your health.

2. Ensure that a competent person supervises the work.

3. Inform you of the significant hazards identified in the risk assessment.

4. The safe way of working will be in a method statement which will be explained to you.

5. At no time place you in danger.

6. Provide you with adequate instruction and training.

What you should do for your site and employer

1. Follow the agreed safe system of work.

2. Not take risks with your or anyone else's health or safety.

3. Report any aspect of your work which you feel is unsafe.

4. Comply with any permit systems which are in operation.

F
18

Introduction

Plumbing and gas-related work is highly specialised and potentially dangerous. All such work must be properly planned, only carried out by trained and competent contractors and adequately supervised as necessary.

No-one should attempt to work on any gas pipework or equipment unless they are a Gas Safe registered engineer.

 Poorly thought out or executed gas-related work activities can kill.

Safe methods of working

Safe working must include giving due attention and:

☑ looking after equipment and hand tools to ensure they are safe to use, including carrying out simple repairs (such as replacing a split file handle) where this is practical

☑ being aware that cutting large diameter pipes will leave extremely sharp insides to the pipe

☑ leaving all places of work in a safe condition if they have to be left unoccupied, particularly if working in domestic premises where the occupier may not be risk-aware

☑ ensuring safe access to any place of work and that the workplace itself is safe to occupy (for example using a ladder or stepladder if accessing the loft space of a domestic premises and ensuring that there is safe foot access over the joists)

☑ carrying out the transportation of people, equipment and materials in a safe and responsible manner, such as:

  − only carrying people in the back of a van if it is fitted with factory-fitted seats and seatbelts

  − carrying long lengths of tubing in a pipe-rack attached to the roof of a van

  − always wearing a seat belt, when one is provided, if driving construction plant

☑ if the sides of an excavation are not supported and show signs of collapse, it must not be entered by any person.

 Readers of this chapter should also refer to the 'Common elements' section of Chapter F23 HVACR.

F
18

Plumbing or gas

F
18

19

Highway works

What your site and employer should do for you

1. Develop safe methods which offer you maximum protection from road users and hazards.

2. Train you if you work on any live highway.

3. Train you if you operate mobile plant or equipment.

4. Provide, maintain and service the correct plant and equipment.

5. Provide the correct PPE for tasks and high-visibility clothing for the road type.

What you should do for your site and employer

1. Follow the step-by-step safe system of work and site or highway traffic rules.

2. Position signs and cones in the right sequence in the correct place.

3. Wear your task PPE (high-visibility clothing, seat belts, and so on) at all times.

4. Do not work in the safety zone and do not use hand signals to control traffic.

5. Report any defects and promptly complete any required daily and weekly inspections.

F
19

Signing, lighting and guarding

The working environment on the highway will involve you working with, or alongside, pedestrians and moving traffic and will lead to problems rising from confusion, conflict and delays.

To reduce this, a clear and concise **signing, lighting and guarding** procedure must be put in place.

Temporary traffic management (TTM) forms the basis of warning, informing and directing the pedestrian and the road user, through and round the site, by the means of signs, cones, and barriers. Most of the common situations are described in the Code of Practice *(Safety at Street Works and Road Works) – the Red book.* Further advice can be found in Chapter 8 of the *Traffic signs manual.*

Safe works – basic principles

☑ To comply with health and safety legislation, a risk assessment will need to have been done to ensure that a safe system of work, in respect to signing, lighting and guarding, is in place at all times.

☑ It is your responsibility to sign, guard, light and maintain your works safely.

☑ It is management's responsibility to provide the equipment in good condition – it is your responsibility to use it in the correct way.

☑ You will need to wear high-visibility clothing whether visiting or working on the site.

☑ Signs, lights and guarding equipment should be secured by bags of granular material placed at low level, to avoid them being moved by wind or passing traffic.

☑ Check regularly, at least once every day, that signs and cones have not been moved, and have not become damaged or dirty.

☑ Drivers must be able to see the advance warning signs. Where visibility is poor, or there are obstructions, additional signs should be provided. Signs should be set out for traffic approaching from all possible directions.

☑ You may have to duplicate warning signs on both sides of the road (for example where signs on the left-hand side are obscured by heavy traffic).

☑ You must include the works area, working space and safety zone in the area to be marked off with cones (and lamps if necessary). Never use a safety zone as a work or storage area.

☑ If there are temporary footways in the carriageway, or obstructions (such as stored materials or plant, not already within the working space), sign and guard them separately to the same standard.

☑ In many cases traffic control will be necessary.

☑ Traffic conditions may change from those expected and adjustments may be needed. If in doubt consult your supervisor.

☑ On completion of the works, ensure that all plant, equipment and materials are removed promptly from the site. All signs, lighting and guarding equipment must be removed immediately when they are no longer needed – it is a legal requirement.

F
19

Site layout

The site layout consists of the following:

- ☑ advance signing – length depends on the speed and type of road
- ☑ works area
- ☑ working space
- ☑ safety zone comprising:
  - the lead-in taper
  - longways clearance
  - sideways clearance
  - exit taper.

The safety zone is provided to protect you from the traffic and to protect the traffic from you. You may only enter it to maintain cones and other road signs. Materials and equipment must not be placed in it. The sideways clearance is the space between the working space and the moving traffic and varies with the speed limit. If pedestrians are diverted into the carriageway, you must provide a safety zone between the outer pedestrian barrier and the traffic. If the carriageway width does not permit the full sideways clearance you must consult your supervisor. It may be necessary to divert traffic or reduce speeds to below 10 mph.

 Don't work in the safety zone – you may lose more than your hat.

Setting out the site

You are at greatest risk when setting out the site, so:

- ☑ switch on your flashing beacon(s)
- ☑ stop the vehicle in a safe place
- ☑ put on your high-visibility clothing
- ☑ get out of the vehicle on the passenger side where possible
- ☑ observe traffic movement at all times
- ☑ position signs in the correct sequence, at the correct distance and where they can be seen clearly – they must not cause a hazard to pedestrians
- ☑ secure the signs with sandbags
- ☑ check that the signing is correct before starting work.

F
19

Other considerations

Pedestrian movement

Footway working may mean the re-routing of pedestrians. You may need to provide a temporary footway, minimum width as specified by the Code of Practice, using barriers (with tapping rails for the blind or partially sighted), ramps and information signs.

Works vehicles

All works vehicles should be of a conspicuous colour and must have an amber warning beacon. Any vehicle wishing to enter a site must switch on the amber beacon. This reduces the risk of having been followed into the site by private vehicles; should this occur you will need to assist the driver to leave the site via the nearest designated exit.

Motorways and high speed dual carriageways (50 mph and above)

Extra precautions are necessary, including the following:

- ☑ long sleeved high-visibility clothing must be worn

- ☑ advance warning signs need to be duplicated on the central reservation

- ☑ all traffic management must be undertaken by a registered traffic management contractor

- ☑ if you are entering a site on a motorway, you must switch on your flashing amber beacon and the appropriate indicator approximately 200 m before the access point, in order to give following traffic sufficient advance warning.

Short stop/mobile working operations

These include continuous mobile operations (such as hedge trimming), as well as those which involve movement with periodic stops (for example gully emptying) and short duration works (for example pothole filling). This work must only be carried out where there is good visibility and during periods of low risk (such as light traffic).

The basic requirements for the works vehicle are:

- ☑ it must be conspicuously coloured

- ☑ it must have one or more roof-mounted amber flashing beacons operating

- ☑ a keep right/left arrow sign must be displayed on or at the rear of the vehicle, showing drivers approaching on the same side of the carriageway which side to pass. This directional sign must be covered or removed when travelling to and from the site.

This is the minimum traffic management required for short stop/mobile operations.

Advance warning signs are necessary when there is not enough space for two-way traffic to pass the works vehicle or where it cannot be seen clearly. The signs may be placed up to one mile from the works vehicle.

F
19

Traffic control systems

Under no circumstances should you use hand signals to control traffic. Only the police are legally allowed to do this.

The *Red book* describes the various systems, where and when they may be installed, and should be consulted in all cases.

Give and take

- ☑ Speed limit 30 mph or less.
- ☑ Coned off area 50 m or less.
- ☑ Drivers approaching the works can see at least 50 m beyond the end of the works.
- ☑ Traffic, including heavy goods vehicles, is very light.

Priority signs

- ☑ Coned off area 80 m or less.
- ☑ Drivers approaching the works can see at least 60 m beyond the end of the coned area for 30 mph speed limit. Other distances are given for different speed limits.
- ☑ Two-way traffic flow is light.

Stop/go boards

- ☑ Works length can be up to 500 m depending on two-way traffic flow levels.
- ☑ Normally use stop/go boards at each end of the works.
- ☑ Where visibility is impeded, a communication system must be employed.
- ☑ Allow sufficient time for traffic to clear with both boards showing 'stop'.
- ☑ Consult your supervisor if the works are near a railway level crossing or a road junction.

Portable traffic signals (temporary traffic lights)

- ☑ Works length can normally be up to 300 m.
- ☑ Signals must be put up and removed in an organised manner and specific sequence. The Department of Transport's booklet, *An introduction to the use of vehicle actuated portable traffic signals* (the *Pink book*), provides detailed guidance.
- ☑ Allow more time for slow-moving traffic, cyclists and horse riders, by increasing the all-red timings.
- ☑ Most sites will only need one set of signal heads – where visibility is poor a double-headed system should be used.
- ☑ Where signal cables cross the carriageway, cable protectors must be used and the signs ramp/ramp ahead must be used.
- ☑ If the detector systems become faulty, you must operate the signals on fixed time or manual, and contact the service company or your supervisor.

F
19

Mobile plant

Maintaining mobile plant

If you are an operator you are responsible for daily and weekly maintenance to ensure your plant/equipment is in a safe condition, giving particular attention to:

☑ maintaining wheels and tyres to avoid making handling more difficult and increasing tyre wear. Check condition of tyres, no bald spots, depth of tread, no cuts to side wall, wheel nuts tightened and the 'tell-tales' aligned

☑ maintaining correct tyre pressure as failure could lead to instability and increased or uneven tyre wear

☑ ensuring the horn, flashing beacon, lights and indicators all work

☑ keeping windscreens and mirrors clean and mirrors adjusted for good visibility – this is particularly important when manoeuvring

☑ making sure windscreen wipers and washers operate efficiently, including keeping the washer bottle topped up

☑ checking levels of fuel, oil, water and brake fluids

☑ making sure brakes, including hand/parking brakes, operate efficiently and where air brakes are fitted the air storage tanks must be drained daily

☑ keeping the cab clean, tidy and clear of any loose articles that may obstruct the operation of foot pedals and controls

☑ checking that your clothing, especially if you are a wearing a winter jacket, does not snag on controls/dead man switches.

Diesel must never be used to clean mobile plant or prevent bitumen or asphalt sticking to buckets or load beds, as this will make it very slippery and present a serious risk of injury from slips and falls. Use suitable access equipment to prevent serious injury from falls when hosing down plant, especially for high level or load beds of lorries and gritters.

 Mobile plant in an unsafe condition must not be used.

Operating mobile plant

If you operate plant you must be trained/competent to operate the type of plant you are authorised to use. You should have an appropriate driving licence and/or plant operator's certificate/card. Before operating any plant for the first time, you should read and understand the manufacturer's operating instructions and be familiar with the controls and their function.

☑ You must not work excessive hours (the Drivers' Hours Regulations and the Working Time Directive limit the number of hours that may be worked in any day or week).

☑ Operator and plant record books must be completed where necessary.

☑ You must be aware of the gross vehicle weight, the maximum axle weights and overall dimensions of the plant.

F
19

☑ When refuelling any plant, remember, no smoking or naked lights and switch off the ignition.

☑ You are responsible for the safe operation and condition of your mobile plant at all times.

☑ You must comply with road traffic legislation and site rules where applicable.

☑ The use of an amber beacon does not exempt you from compliance with the Highway Code.

☑ You must stop operations immediately and report defects that present a serious risk to the safe operation of plant (such as faulty controls or 'dead man's handle').

☑ Where fitted, seatbelts must be worn (they could save your life).

☑ Use mirrors and CCTV, if fitted, when manoeuvring.

☑ A signaller must be used when reversing in areas where there may be pedestrians.

☑ Do not operate mobile plant too close to any excavation, no matter how shallow. Stop blocks are the preferred method of preventing mobile plant getting too near to an excavation when tipping.

☑ Obey all speed limit, height restriction, direction and warning signage.

☑ Be alert to the dangers of colliding or clipping scaffolding, temporary works, mobile towers, MEWPs and ladders.

Parking

☑ Where possible, park on level ground in a designated area, clear of pedestrians. Handbrake/parking brake should be on, engine off and key removed.

☑ If you cannot park on level ground you may need to chock the wheels or otherwise prevent unintended movement of the plant.

☑ All hydraulic equipment (such as buckets, forks, back-actors) should be lowered to the rest position.

Access

☑ Only authorised persons should be allowed onto mobile plant.

☑ Passengers may only be carried on mobile plant equipped with sufficient, suitable seating for them.

☑ Wait until the mobile plant has come to a complete stop before getting on and off. Never jump down – always use the steps and grab rails.

☑ Maintain three points of contact with access ladders or hand/foot holds.

☑ Never, at any time, work under an unpropped mobile plant body.

Maintain three points of contact – don't jump down.

The following operations may require detailed consideration and risk assessment to determine safe access:

- ☑ sheeting loads
- ☑ maintenance
- ☑ working at height at the top of the mobile plant
- ☑ anywhere else where falls may be likely.

Loads

Loading and the load are the operator's responsibility.

- ☑ Plant must not be overloaded and loads must be spread evenly and secured.
- ☑ Operators of mobile plant should not remain in the seat or unprotected cab while it is being mechanically loaded.
- ☑ Check sideboards, curtains, sheeting and tailboards are fastened and secure before moving off.
- ☑ Check load for security. Any projections must be properly marked and clearly visible.
- ☑ Care should be taken when removing lashings as the load may have shifted during transit or moved when being released.
- ☑ Loading and unloading of tippers must be attended by a competent banksman.
  Rear end tippers are liable to overturn whilst tipping on uneven or made up ground.
- ☑ Personnel should stay well clear of any tipping or loading operations.
- ☑ Tippers and dumpers must not travel with the body in the raised position after the load has been discharged.

Trailers

Before towing any trailer or plant, you must ensure you have the correct class of driving licence. It is essential to ensure that the driver is licensed for the specific combination (towing vehicle plus trailer and load).

- ☑ The towing vehicle, trailer and compressor must be compatible and any conversions secured with the correct towing pin.
- ☑ When being towed on a highway the trailer must be fitted with registration number plates and rear tail lights.
- ☑ Where fitted, trailer parking brakes must be applied before disconnecting the trailer from the towing vehicle. On slopes, trailer wheels should also be chocked.
- ☑ Trailers fitted with independent operating brakes should be connected to the towing vehicle by a cable, which will activate the trailer's brakes if the tow hitch fails. Otherwise the trailer must be fitted with a safety chain connected to the vehicle.

F
19

 Ratchet straps or similar should not be secured and tightened onto rope hooks, which have no safe working load. Only use designated securing points.

Mobile plant used for lifting

☑ Only authorised and trained operators should operate lifting equipment.

☑ Lifting equipment should get a daily visual check before use.

☑ Lifting equipment must be subject to a recorded weekly inspection.

☑ Lifting accessories (chains, strops, shackles) must be thoroughly examined every six months.

☑ Equipment for lifting persons (such as a scissor lift) must be thoroughly examined every six months.

☑ Other lifting equipment must be thoroughly examined every 12 months.

☑ Care must always be taken when operating extending booms or other lifting equipment near overhead power lines.

☑ The safest method is limiting the boom extension or height of the mast.

The rated safe working load (SWL) of any lifting equipment must never be exceeded.

20

Specialist work at height

What your site and employer should do for you

1. Ensure work at height is properly planned so that your place of work at height and the access route to and from it are safe to occupy.

2. Provide, inspect and maintain the most appropriate work at height equipment.

3. Provide adequate safety equipment to prevent falls, or if necessary to arrest any falls which do occur.

4. Ensure you are trained and regularly updated in methods of working safely at height.

5. Give you a written safe system of work which you fully understand so that you can work at height safely.

What you should do for your site and employer

1. Fully understand and follow the agreed safe system of work (including using any equipment provided to prevent or arrest falls).

2. Report any aspect of your work which you feel is unsafe.

3. Not interfere with anything provided for safety unless you are trained and competent.

4. Not use powered access equipment upon which you have not been trained.

5. Not take risks or short cuts.

6. Report any falls which occur, even if they cause no injury.

F
20

Introduction

☑ Every year many deaths and serious injuries result from falls from height; some are falls from below 2 m.

☑ All too frequently the same types of accidents reoccur (such as falls through fragile roof materials and falls from ladders).

☑ In many cases taking basic safety precautions and/or providing training could have prevented suffering.

It is assumed that you are reading this chapter because you regularly work at height. If so, one of the risk factors, the time spent at working height, is increased. You must be confident that your employer, or you if you are self-employed, has/have taken the necessary steps to ensure that the jobs you do can be carried out without risking the safety of yourself or anyone else.

You should also read Chapter 14 Working at height, which explains what employers and in some cases you must do to comply with the law and keep yourself, and others, safe whilst working at height.

Safe working at height

Safely working at height depends upon:

☑ the job being properly planned (a safe system of work, which follows the hierarchy on page 143)

☑ the people who will carry out the job being adequately trained and competent

☑ the job being carried out in accordance with the safe system of work

☑ adequate supervision being provided, as necessary.

Before you starting working at height (for example on a roof) there are many things that your employer, or you, can do to ensure that the job is carried out safely, for example:

☑ assessing the risks arising from the work and taking measures which will:

 – prevent people or materials falling from height

 – make sure that there are no serious injuries or damage if someone or something does fall

☑ drawing up a method statement that explains exactly how the job should be carried out and making sure that the people doing the job understand it. The method statement should include details of:

 – how falls will be prevented

 – the sequence of operations that must be carried out

 – the equipment to be used

 – who will supervise the job.

If you are not sure that what you have been asked to do is safe or you are unhappy about any other aspect of working at height, you should discuss it with your supervisor.

F
20

Generally, the risks will depend on:

☑ how experienced the people are in doing the job they are required to do

☑ the number of people who will be working at height

☑ the length of time that people will be working at height

☑ the method of access selected to get the people doing the job up to the workplace

☑ the nature of the place of work (such as scaffold platform or leading edge of new roof)

☑ whether or not precautions and a rescue plan are necessary in case something does fall

☑ the weather

☑ the nature of any materials that will have to be hoisted and/or stored at height

☑ the method of hoisting materials

☑ whether or not people can be kept out of the area below where the work is taking place.

Falls are still the biggest killer, but many could have been prevented.

Hierarchy of control

Step 1. Avoid working at height
e.g. assemble on the ground and crane up, use extendable handles on equipment.

Only if this can't be avoided then:

Step 2. Use an existing safe place of work
e.g. parapet walls, defined access points, staircases.

Only if this can't be done then:

Step 3. Provide work equipment to prevent falls
e.g. scaffolding, edge protection, handrails, podiums, mobile towers, MEWPs.

Only if this can't be provided then:

Step 4. Mitigate distance and consequence of a fall
e.g. safety netting, airbags, crash decks

(harnesses must be used as a last resort).

Step 5. Provide instruction, training and/or other means
e.g. PASMA training for mobile towers, IPAF training for MEWPs,

using ladders (the last resort).

Roof work

Much work that is carried out at height involves working on roofs, which can present particular dangers.

- ☑ Fragile roofs are particularly dangerous because it is not always clear at the outset whether or not the roof cladding is a fragile material. A safe system of work must be in place.

- ☑ Anyone who has doubts should consult the risk assessment or the method statement.

- ☑ High-level features (such as overhead cables) present additional dangers.

- ☑ The surface is likely to become slippery after rain, frost, or snow.

- ☑ If you will be working near power cables check with your supervisor or the person in charge of the site that it is safe to be on the roof.

F
20

☑ Fragile roof lights can be dangerous if not barriered-off or covered with securely fixed covers that can withstand any load imposed upon them.

☑ Specialist access equipment is likely to be required for carrying out work above fragile roofs (for example the inspection of pipework).

☑ Materials must be stored on roofs in a safe manner so that:

- the pitch of the roof is taken into account when deciding what can be stored safely
- they cannot fall or be blown off the roof
- during loading-up an excessive 'point loading' is avoided
- they are promptly distributed around the roof to where they are needed
- a safe method of getting them up to the roof is employed (for example inclined hoist, scaffold-hoist, safety pulley or gin-wheel)
- ladders are only used for loading-up lightweight, non-bulky items
- they do not pose a hazard to anyone working on the roof
- they can be accessed safely.

Fall prevention methods

Scaffolds

A common way of preventing falls is to use a secure and stable working platform (such as a scaffold). Below are some essential considerations when using scaffolds.

☑ Is it a safe and suitable means of access for the job that has to be done (for example are the lift heights satisfactory)?

☑ They must only be erected, altered and dismantled by a person who is trained and competent. The scaffolder should hold a current CISRS card.

☑ Be particularly watchful for unauthorised modifications to system scaffolds.

☑ Each working platform must be wide enough to allow the job to be carried out safely and for the passage of people and equipment as necessary.

☑ Never overload working platforms, as this has been the cause of many scaffold collapses.

☑ Anyone who is **not** trained and competent must never interfere with a scaffold, (for example by removing a tie or guard-rail which is in their way).

☑ Where someone could be injured by a fall from a working platform or hit by falling objects, edge protection must be fitted to the working platforms.

☑ Every scaffold must be inspected periodically by a competent person, with the findings of the inspection entered in a register. Details may also be recorded on a plastic tag, usually fixed to the scaffold adjacent to the access point.

☑ If you think that any aspect of a scaffold is not as it should be, immediately report it to someone in authority.

F 20

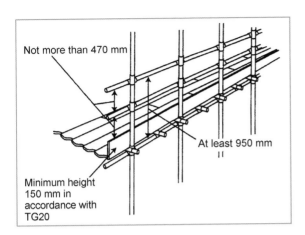

Mobile elevating work platform

Common types of mobile elevating work platform (MEWP) are cherry pickers and scissor lifts. Safety considerations when using a MEWP are shown below.

☑ You must not operate any type of MEWP unless you are trained, competent and authorised. Holding an IPAF card is a good indication.

☑ Users of cherry pickers must normally wear a safety harness and restraint (short) lanyard secured to the designated anchorage point.

☑ It must allow safe access to the place of work. If it does not quite reach, a bigger machine is necessary. Do not stand on the guard-rails or put a stepladder or hop up on the working platform.

☑ The ground-level controls must only be used in an emergency (for example if the operator becomes ill or is trapped).

Note: in the event of an emergency, a responsible person on the ground should know where to find and use the lowering controls (sometimes indicated by the IPAF symbol shown here).

☑ There must be a rescue plan in place in case the operator becomes incapacitated and cannot lower the working platform.

☑ Before elevating the machine, operators must identify any projections or other features on the structure which could trap them between the guard-rails and the structure.

☑ Operators must know how to carry out daily and weekly checks.

☑ A MEWP must not be used as a substitute for the stairs in the structure being worked upon. Never carry more than the maximum safe load in a MEWP (the maximum load in terms of kilogrammes or number of people will be displayed on a plate somewhere on the machine).

☑ The person planning the job must make sure that a survey is carried out to identify any underground voids (such as drains or cellars) which could collapse under the load.

☑ Only use MEWPs where the ground is solid enough to take the weight.

☑ Operators must be aware of the wind-loading on a raised MEWP and be prepared to stop work and lower the machine if the wind speed is judged to be too high.

☑ Forecasts of wind speed, as measured on the Beaufort Scale, can be obtained before starting the job.

☑ The Beaufort Scale categorises the wind strength as being between Force 0 and Force 12; the higher the number the higher the wind-speed (for example Force 2 is a light breeze and Force 7 is a near gale).

Access towers

Access towers can be:

☑ mobile or static, depending if wheels are fitted

☑ built from tube and fitting scaffold components or more commonly prefabricated alloy frames which 'slot together'.

Tube and fitting towers must only be erected, altered or dismantled by a trained and competent scaffolder (for example someone who holds a CISRS card).

Alloy towers must only be built, altered or dismantled, in accordance with the manufacturers' instructions, by someone who has been trained and is competent on that type of tower (for example someone who holds a PASMA card).

Safety considerations when using a tower are:

☑ the guard-rails and toe-boards must have been fitted before the tower is used

☑ some types of alloy towers have guard-rails which can be positioned before the working platform is accessed

☑ the brakes must be on at all times that a mobile tower is not being moved

☑ the ground or floor surface must be level and sufficiently firm to take the loading of the base plates (static) or wheels (mobile)

☑ a mobile tower must not be moved whilst anyone or any equipment is on the platform

☑ once the platform of a mobile tower has been occupied the trapdoor must be closed immediately to prevent anyone or anything falling through it

**F
20**

☑ the working platform must only be accessed by using the built-in ladder (**never** climb up the outside of a tower or use a free-standing ladder)

☑ provision must be made for the safe hoisting of tools and materials up onto the platform

☑ every tower must be inspected periodically by a trained, competent and authorised person, including an inspection after any event that is likely to have made it unsafe to use (such as impact by a vehicle or being subjected to severe wind or weather).

Ladders and stepladders

More stable items of access equipment are often now used for some jobs that, at one time, would have been carried out using a ladder or stepladder. However, they can still be used for access to places of work at height and for carrying out light work of short duration where the risk of a fall is low. A properly carried out risk assessment will show whether a ladder or stepladder is an appropriate item of access equipment to use. for any particular job.

Some factors which must be considered if you are going to use a ladder or stepladder are:

☑ possible defects, including splits in the material (from which the equipment is manufactured), missing or distorted rungs or frayed, broken or missing tie-cords (stepladders only)

☑ ensure that any ladder extends at least 1 m (five rungs) above the stepping-off point if there is not an alternative handhold

☑ ensure that where a ladder is used for access to a high-level platform or similar, there is a landing at least every 9 m (about 30 foot) that the ladder rises vertically

☑ any ladder used on site must have been manufactured for heavy industrial use and it will be labelled 'Class 1' or 'BS EN 131'; any ladder labelled 'Class 2' (light trade) or 'Class 3' (domestic use only) means that it is not suitable for use on a construction site

☑ various fittings are available that enable ladders to be used safely, such as:
  – anti-slip mats and other anti-slip devices upon which the styles are positioned
  – adjustable stabilisers to prevent sideways slipping
  – adjustable extensions to enable use on sloping ground
  – stand-off frames that avoid the need to rest ladders against fragile or flexible materials (such as plastic guttering)
  – ridge-hooks that enable an ordinary ladder to be converted to a roof ladder

☑ ladders are made from various materials:
  – generally alloy ladders are lighter than wooden ones but will conduct electricity and so cannot be used close to live overhead cables
  – fibreglass ladders are non-conducting and so are safer to use adjacent to electrical supplies
  – all types of ladder will conduct electricity if they are wet

☑ if planning to use a roof ladder:
  – it must be purpose made or a normal ladder fitted with a proprietary fitting
  – a stable working platform at eaves height will provide safe access to the roof ladder with the added comfort factor of edge protection

**F
20**

- as a minimum, 'catch-barriers' at eaves height will provide protection against falls
- if using a leaning ladder for access, the transition between ladders must be safe
- a leaning ladder used for access must be stable and extend 1 m above eaves height
- consider whether a roof scaffold is a better option

☑ if planning to use an extending ladder:

- keep the minimum overlap between sections as specified in the manufacturer's instructions
- the latching mechanism (and hoisting rope/fittings if appropriate) must be part of the pre-use inspection
- the length/weight of the ladder and how many people will be raising it will determine whether it is safer to extend the ladder before raising it
- if extending it after raising it, be aware of overhead obstructions.

Before work (such as erecting specialist modular scaffold anchored frames, using anchor bolts/inserts) checks must be carried out, including:

☑ making sure that the modular frames and components are sound

☑ testing the inserted anchor bolts/inserts to ensure capability of a structure to take the designed loads

☑ making sure that everyone involved is wearing a safety harness and suitable fall arrest systems are in place.

Preventing falling objects

One of the obvious dangers of working at height is the possibility of materials, equipment, hand tools, and so on being dropped or thrown onto anyone below. Measures that should be taken to prevent this include:

☑ being aware of the presence of people, including the public, below the work area

☑ rigging a safety net, overlaid with a fine-mesh debris to prevent falling tools and materials from reaching the ground

☑ consider fitting a short lanyard with a wrist-loop to hand tools

☑ fitting edge protection to the working platforms of scaffolds

☑ wearing a chin-strap with a safety helmet to prevent it falling off if leaning over an exposed edge

☑ storing materials awaiting use in a safe manner away from the edges of flat roofs

☑ using a waste chute, with the bottom just above a skip, to transfer waste materials to a lower level.

F 20

Fall arrest (protecting you if you do fall)

Health and safety law recognises that there will be situations where physical barriers cannot be used, and the use of collective fall arrest measures (such as safety nets or air-bags) is not practical. In these circumstances individual fall arrest measures (such as harness and lanyards may be used).

Factors to be considered when you or your employer selects fall arrest measures, are:

☑ collective fall arrest systems, (such as safety nets or air-bags), which are preferable to personal protective measures (such as a harness and lanyard)

☑ a safety harness and lanyard should only be used in situations where:

 – it is not practical to use other fall arrest measures (such as a safety net or air bags)

 – a purpose-designed, secure anchor point is available (integral or mobile anchor)

 – users have been trained in the pre-use inspection, fitting and use of the equipment

 – users are aware that any damaged equipment must not be used

 – work must be planned to avoid a 'pendulum' effect if someone does fall

 – users can select the correct lanyard for the job (restraint or shock-absorbing)

 – a rescue plan is in place to reduce to a minimum the time that someone is suspended in a harness: trauma and even death can result from not doing so

☑ essential features of any harness used are:

 – it must be a full body harness that keeps someone who has fallen in an upright position until rescued (BE EN 361)

 – ideally it will be fitted with a feature that enables the fallen person to raise their thighs above horizontal or to 'stand up' whilst awaiting rescue, releasing the pressure caused by the leg straps and reducing the chances of suspension trauma

 – it must be inspected before use, with more detailed inspections at periods specified by the manufacturer.

Safety nets

If safety nets are used:

☑ they will be rigged immediately below where people are working to minimise the height of any fall

☑ they must only be rigged by someone who is trained, competent and authorised to do so

☑ work must stop if any damage to the net is discovered and the damage must be reported

☑ materials or debris that have fallen into the net must be cleared from it promptly

☑ no-one other than a trained and competent net rigger, should interfere with the securing cords. If you find one is in your way report the problem

☑ they are often rigged using mobile elevating work platforms (MEWPs) and so the floor surface must be suitable and able to withstand the loading

☑ if MEWPs cannot be used it may be necessary to employ competent rope-access technicians to rig the nets (for example IRATA trained)

F
20

☑ nets must be periodically inspected and any damaged nets replaced

☑ net repairs must only be carried out by a trained and competent person.

Air-bags/bean bags

These are a very effective method of arresting falls, if they are installed correctly. They are generically known as *soft-landing systems*.

If they are used:

☑ they must be supplied and installed by competent contractors

☑ they must be clipped together as necessary to provide a continuous fall protection area

☑ air bag inflation pumps must be kept running whenever anyone is working above them

☑ they must fill the area over which fall arrest protection is required

☑ air bags must not be too big; if over-size they will exert a sideways pressure on anything that is confining them as they inflate

☑ care must be taken to ensure that anyone who falls cannot bounce or slide onto another hazard (for example onto exposed rebar or out of a first floor window).

Rope access

☑ Rope access is a very specialised activity requiring particular skills and training.

☑ Anyone engaged to carry out rope access must be IRATA or similar industry trained (Industrial Rope Access Trade Association).

☑ Generally, rope access is required where it is impractical to provide a working platform, other fall prevention methods or fall arrest measures.

☑ Tasks that rope access can be used for include:

- structural surveys
- non-destructive testing
- localised concrete repairs
- cladding/glazing panel replacement

- secondary fixings
- surface preparation and decorating
- concrete spraying
- pressure pointing.

F
20

21

Lifts and escalators

What your site and employer should do for you

1.	Ensure that a competent person plans and supervises the work.
2.	Provide you with a method of working that is safe and without risks to your health.
3.	The safe way of working will be in a method statement and risk assessment which will be explained to you.
4.	Provide you with the right tools and equipment for the job.
5.	Provide you with adequate information, instruction and training.

What you should do for your site and employer

1.	Follow the agreed safe system of work.
2.	Use only equipment and methods you have been trained in.
3.	Wear the right PPE for the task.
4.	Not take risks or short cuts.
5.	Stop and seek advice if anything changes or seems unsafe.

F
21

Lifts and escalators

By the nature of the equipment, work on lifts and escalators can be extremely hazardous and must only be undertaken by trained and competent personnel.

The actual requirements for this training and competence are detailed in Code of Practices BS 7255 *Safe working on lifts* **and BS 7801** *Safe working on escalators and moving walks in use.*

The Lift and Escalator Industry Association (LEIA), which is responsible for the lift and escalator specialist section, represents most of the lift and escalator companies in the UK and its members are committed to the LEIA safety charter which requires member companies to work in accordance with BS 7255 and BS 7801 and to ensure, in particular, that all their employees will:

☑ protect themselves and others from falls and falling objects

☑ use and verify **stop** and other devices when accessing, egressing and working on car tops and in lift and escalator pits to ensure total control of the equipment

☑ electrically isolate and lock off, when power is not required and when working close to unguarded machinery.

These are just three essential control measures that must be operated to ensure safe working.

For further guidance refer to:

The Lift and Escalator Industry Association
33-34 Devonshire Street
London
W1G 6PY

Tel: 020 7935 3013
Fax: 020 7935 3321

www.leia.co.uk

F
21

Lifts and escalators

22

Tunnelling

What your site and employer should do for you

1. Ensure that a competent person plans and supervises the work.

2. Provide you with a method of working that is safe and without risks to your health.

3. The safe way of working will be in a method statement and risk assessment which will be explained to you.

4. Provide you with the right tools and equipment for the job.

5. Provide you with adequate information, instruction and training.

What you should do for your site and employer

1. Follow the agreed safe system of work.

2. Use only equipment and methods you have been trained in.

3. Wear the right PPE for the task.

4. Do not take risks or short cuts.

5. Stop and seek advice if anything changes or seems unsafe.

F
22

Introduction

Due to the nature of tunnelling, where people are often working far underground and a long way from a place of safety into the open air, the importance of working in a manner which is safe and free of risks to health cannot be overemphasised.

The following text highlights some of the common potential hazards that could be experienced during tunnelling operations. The risk control measures and safe systems of work identified follow BS 6164, which is the Code of Practice for health and safety in tunnelling in the construction industry.

Safe systems of work

Formal safe systems of work are essential during tunnelling operations. Examples are:

☑ ensuring continuous structural stability by immediately installing supports to excavated ground

☑ ensuring that where a shaft is being constructed, provision is made for:
   – ventilation
   – continuous gas monitoring
   – adequate guarding

☑ using compressed air tunnelling, where necessary, to prevent or reduce the ingress of water during tunnel construction

☑ using a water-spray curtain to help reduce the movement of smoke through a tunnel

☑ ensuring that personal protective equipment (PPE), safety signs and notices and a rescue plan are provided

☑ ensuring that the safe system of work for track maintenance workers and locomotive drivers, includes provision for:
   – a lookout person
   – flashing lights either side of the work area
   – everyone involved in the job wearing high-visibility clothing
   – a permit to work
   – adequate refuge space

☑ appreciating that falling objects or failure of the load is the greatest danger from suspended loads during shaft sinking operations

☑ storing tunnel segments in a secure manner that prevents:
   – falling or collapse
   – any other movement
   – instability

F
22

☑ protecting against the rebound or fall of materials during and after sprayed concrete operations

☑ taking great care to ensure that oxygen cylinders do not come into contact with grease, to avoid potential explosions

☑ wearing a safety harness when building rings from a platform within a shaft.

Communication

Effective communication is essential for safe tunnelling operations. For this reason, the power supply for communications equipment must be independent of the mains power supply so that it continues working if the mains power fails.

The most common form of communication between the surface and the tunnelling face is either by radio or a tannoy system.

Workers should not be allowed to work alone in tunnels because they may not be able to communicate to others if they had an accident or became unwell.

It is also important that you report any defects (such as torn ventilation ducting) to a supervisor as soon as possible.

Safe access and egress

Safely getting to and from a place of work is equally as important as working safely whilst there.

Some factors to consider are:

☑ fitting secure barriers of at least 1.2 m in height around every shaft, to prevent falls

☑ every working shaft must have a minimum of two escape methods or routes from each place where people are working

☑ a tally system must be in place to control entry and exit to any tunnel under construction

☑ vertical ladders in tunnel shafts must have a landing (resting place) every 6 m

☑ safety nets and/or sliding doors must be fitted to man-riding cages/hoists/baskets to prevent anyone falling out or leaning out whilst it is in motion

☑ man-riding cages must not be overloaded: A label or notice will state the maximum number of people that can be carried

☑ water must not be allowed to accumulate above rail level in a tunnel for maintenance purposes

☑ the maximum distance between safe refuges in a tunnel is:
  – 50 m – straight sections
  – 25 m – curved sections.

F
22

Emergency actions

In effect tunnels are confined spaces requiring, in most cases, that a self-rescue set is made available to each worker. Where one is provided, you should be aware that:

☑ it must be immediately available at all times

☑ the duration of the air supply will be significantly reduced if you exert yourself whilst wearing it (such as when running)

☑ at best the air supply will only last for 20 minutes.

In an emergency the rescue services will use the 'tally-board' to establish who is underground. A tally system counts people in and people out.

In the event of an emergency or fire, if possible raise the alarm, and if safe to do so leave the tunnel.

If the ventilation system alarm activates you should immediately evacuate the workplace.

Fire and hot works

An underground fire can have devastating consequences. The close control of fire risks is essential, therefore:

☑ smoking, or even the carrying of smoking materials, is not permitted underground

☑ smoking or other naked flames are not permitted within 10 m of battery charging areas because of the flammable gas produced by lead-acid batteries when they are charging

☑ hot works are not permitted within 10 m of any diesel fuelling point

☑ fire checks must be maintained for at least 60 minutes after hot works have ceased.

Electrical safety

Emergency lighting, which must come on if the main lighting fails, must be installed in tunnels. The maximum distance between emergency lighting units is 50 m.

For personal safety, apart from battery-operated tools, all powered hand tools must operate from a 110 volt supply.

Industrial electrical plugs and sockets are colour coded to indicate what voltage they are carrying:

☑ yellow – 110 volt

☑ blue – 230 volt

☑ red – 415 volt.

F
22

Atmosphere

In tunnelling a safe, breathable atmosphere cannot always be guaranteed unless appropriate control measures are taken, as highlighted below.

The use of appropriate equipment is essential to avoid hazards, such as:

☑ using intrinsically safe (spark proof) electrical and other equipment to prevent igniting potentially explosive atmospheres

☑ **not** using petrol-powered equipment at any time to avoid a lethal build-up of carbon monoxide

☑ only using diesel-powered plant that is fitted with a **fixed** fire extinguishing system.

Maintaining a satisfactory level of oxygen in the air is essential. Usually there is 21% oxygen in the air we breathe. Oxygen deficiency, which causes breathlessness, occurs if the level falls below 19%.

There are potential dangers from other gases that may be found underground:

☑ exposure to **hydrogen sulphide** can kill through respiratory paralysis, however it smells like rotten eggs and so its presence should be immediately obvious

☑ **methane** is explosive and it can displace the oxygen in the air, causing oxygen deficiency

☑ exposure to **carbon monoxide** prevents the intake of oxygen into the body

☑ **nitrogen oxide**, which is generated by diesel-powered equipment, can cause breathing problems.

The use of a calibrated gas detector is a reliable way of detecting the presence of methane and carbon monoxide underground, if the risk of exposure cannot be eliminated.

Forced ventilation is one way of preventing the build up of hazardous gases underground. The failure of ventilation equipment must:

☑ be indicated by an audible alarm

☑ result in an immediate evacuation of the workplace.

Health risks

Tunnelling work will sometimes involve working in a compressed air environment. Decompression illness, often shortened to DCI, is a potential health risk.

Each batching plant must be equipped with an eyewash station to enable the prompt treatment of anyone who suffers from the splatter of concrete on their face.

The following health risks are associated with sprayed concrete linings:

☑ cement burns

☑ hand-arm vibration syndrome

☑ inhalation of dust.

F
22

The following health risks are associated with hand-mining:

☑ vibrating hand tools   ☑ inhalation of dust

☑ noise   ☑ falling mined materials.

Hand-arm vibration syndrome is caused when the safe usage time of vibrating tools are exceeded. The symptoms, which include damage to the nerves and blood vessels in the hand, cannot be cured.

Equipment and moving plant

The movement or operation of plant in close proximity to where people are working will create a potentially dangerous situation unless a safe separation is maintained. Working in the confines of a tunnel can make this difficult to achieve. Here are some examples of good practice:

☑ Crush zones caused by moving plant will be indicated by:
- – signs or barriers
- – flashing warning lights.

☑ All conveyors must be fitted with:
- – an emergency stop system (pull cord or button)
- – an audible alarm to indicate that it is about to start.

☑ Inclined conveyors must be fitted with an anti roll-back device to prevent the belt running backwards due to power loss.

☑ Ensuring that segment erectors have a fail-safety device to stop the operation if the equipment:
- – suffers any malfunction
- – develops a leak
- – suffers a power supply failure.

☑ Fitting audible and/or visible alarms to rams and erectors of tunnel boring machines or hydraulic jacking rams in pipe-jacking shafts/pits, to warn when they are moving.

☑ An alternative control point is the most effective way of overcoming the restricted vision of tunnel boring machine operators during the building process.

☑ Always using a hop up or refuge in a tunnel when vehicles are passing.

☑ Always proceeding immediately to a hop up or refuge if a locomotive or other vehicle is approaching.

☑ The lights fitted to locomotives must be:
- – visible at a minimum distance of 60 m
- – white (if fitted) to the front of the locomotive
- – red (if fitted) to the rear of the locomotive.

☑ Secondary couplings must be fitted to un-braked rolling stock to reduce the risk of it running away.

☑ In an emergency a locomotive must be able to stop with a distance not exceeding 60 m.

F
22

☑ Ideally, the movement of locomotives when entering the back of a tunnel boring machine will be controlled by:

 – traffic lights

 – closed circuit television (CCTV) in the cab.

☑ The traffic light system used to control plant movement underground is:

 – **red** – stop

 – amber – out bye

 – **green** – in bye.

Pipework, services and hoses under pressure

All services running through the tunnel should be safely positioned to avoid them being damaged. The use of pressure systems is potentially hazardous unless safe work practices are adopted, such as:

☑ isolating or releasing stored energy before disconnecting or uncoupling tunnel services

☑ being aware that pumped grouting and sprayed concrete operations can result in:

 – injury resulting from burst hoses

 – hearing damage and loss through excessive noise

 – injury resulting from blowout at the injection point.

☑ immediately releasing the pressure if a grouting or sprayed concrete hose becomes blocked

☑ cleaning grouting pipelines after use to prevent blockages and bursting when they are used again

☑ replacing hoses that show signs of swelling, which indicates they are damaged

☑ fitting anti-whip devices across flexible hose connections to prevent the ends flying about if they become disconnected under pressure

☑ including isolation arrangements in the safe system of work for maintenance work on grouting or slurry lines, especially if removing guards

☑ being aware that hoses which are of a similar size, but with different markings, are **not** interchangeable: Although appearing similar, they could:

 – be of different physical sizes

 – have different operating capacities

 – be for different applications.

F
22

23

Heating, ventilation, air conditioning and refrigeration (HVACR)

What your site and employer should do for you

1. Provide you with a method of working that is safe and without risks to your health.

2. Ensure that a competent person will supervise the work.

3. Inform you of the significant hazards identified in the risk assessment.

4. The safe way of working will be in a method statement which will be explained to you.

5. At no time expect you to work unsafely or work in a place of danger.

6. Provide you with adequate instruction and training.

What you should do for your site and employer

1. Follow the agreed safe system of work.

2. Not take risks with your or anyone else's health or safety.

3. Report any aspect of your work which you feel is unsafe.

4. Comply with any permit systems that are in operation.

F
23

Introduction

Common HVACR elements below should be read by people from the following trades:

- [x] domestic heating and plumbing services (HAPS)

- [x] pipefitting and welding (PFW)

- [x] ductwork (DUCT)

- [x] refrigeration and air conditioning (RAAC)

- [x] services and facilities maintenance (SAF).

You should also read the section later in the chapter that refers to your particular trade.

Common HVACR elements

Competency

Competency is essential if work is to be carried out in a manner which is safe and free of risks to health. Competency can be defined as a blend of skills, training, attitude, knowledge and experience.

Competency is a 'two-way street' in that:

- [x] no-one should ask any other person to carry out a job unless they are known to be competent to carry it out in a manner that is safe and without risks to health

- [x] no person should be prepared to accept any job unless they know that they are competent to carry it out in a manner that is safe and without risks to health.

Other examples of competency are:

- [x] all work must be properly planned in advance with the risks assessed and allowed for

- [x] only Gas Safe registered engineers are allowed to work on gas pipework or components

- [x] dangerous gas fittings that could cause a death or major injury must be reported to the Health and Safety Executive

- [x] the pressure testing of pipework and vessels must only be carried out by someone who has been trained and is competent

- [x] all power tools must be used in a safe and responsible manner

- [x] the side of a cutting-off disc must never be used for grinding and anyone doing so must be stopped immediately

- [x] only competent, trained persons who work for an F-gas registered company are allowed to install, service or maintain systems that contain or are designed to contain refrigerant gasses

- [x] anyone who is concerned over their or anyone else's health or safety must be able to report it to someone in authority on the site.

F
23

Hot work

Hot work presents the obvious risk of fires on site unless the risks are managed: many serious fires have occurred on sites because they were not. For example, anyone carrying out hot work that involves the use of a blowtorch must:

☑ make sure that a fire extinguisher of the correct type is available in the immediate area

☑ remove lagging from pipework for at least 1 m either side of where work will be carried out on lagged pipes

☑ stop any work involving the use of a blowtorch at least one hour before leaving the job and inspect the area before leaving

☑ use a mat of a non-combustible material when a blowtorch is used near to any combustible materials (such as timber).

Anyone planning hot works must implement a hot-work permit scheme and make sure it is followed.

Checking, installing, testing and commissioning installations

☑ Plant and equipment must be installed, tested and commissioned in a manner so that it is safe to use.

☑ It is essential that the unauthorised use of plant and equipment is prevented, if necessary by the locking off of switches and valves, until such time as it has been fully commissioned.

Confined spaces and risers

Confined space working is recognised as being particularly hazardous, particularly if one person is working on their own.

☑ No-one should enter a confined space unless:
  – a risk assessment has been carried out
  – a method statement has been prepared
  – a permit to work system is in place.

☑ Alternative ways of doing the job must always be investigated before entry is made.

☑ Carrying out confined space working in an unsafe manner has been the cause of many deaths, many by people who were trying to rescue other victims.

☑ If natural gas is detected in any occupied confined space (such as an underground service duct), it must be evacuated immediately.

☑ Forced-air mechanical ventilation must be provided where there is insufficient breathable air and RPE is not available.

☑ If oxyacetylene equipment must be used in a confined space, the two main safety considerations are the risks of:
  – unburnt oxygen causing an oxygen enriched atmosphere
  – a flammable gas leak.

☑ Failure of the lighting in a confined space must be guarded against by issuing workers with torches.

F
23

☑ The use of hazardous substances, which can be breathed in, must be closely controlled in confined spaces.

Electrical safety

Electricity can be a killer. It cannot be detected by any of the senses except touch. Working close to live exposed equipment or circuits could result in a fatal shock. Here are some examples of good practice in electrical safety.

☑ Defective electrical equipment, including hand tools, must be taken out of service immediately and a procedure put in place to ensure they cannot be used.

☑ Extension leads must be run in a safe manner so that they are not a tripping hazard. If possible run them above head height or along the join of the walls and the floor.

☑ Electrical distribution circuits must only be installed by competent and authorised electrical contractors.

☑ If the supply system does not meet your needs, tell someone and then stop work until an authorised supply has been installed.

☑ All mains (240 volt) and 110 volt equipment must be periodically tested for electrical safety, commonly known as 'PAT testing'.

☑ Battery-powered tools do not need PAT testing although any mains-powered battery chargers do.

☑ Temporary continuity bonding must be installed before breaking into metal pipework to provide a continuous earth for the installation throughout the duration of the work.

☑ Only battery-powered hand tools should be used to carry out work outside in wet weather.

☑ Testing for concealed cables within the structure of a wall should be carried out, using a cable tracer, before disturbing the fabric of the wall.

☑ Before working on electrically powered equipment:
 – ensure the equipment is switched off
 – isolate the supply at the main board
 – lock and tag out the circuit at the main supply board
 – test the circuit.

☑ If work has to be carried out on electrical equipment and the main isolator does not have a lock out device, the person(s) doing the job should:
 – withdraw and retain the fuses
 – display a clear warning sign on the isolator.

☑ If working near to live exposed conductors is unavoidable, a permit to work system must be put in place because most appliances and equipment run on mains voltage (240 volts).

☑ 110 volt power tools are used on site because they are safer; transformers are used to reduce the 240 volt supply to 110 volts.

☑ Electrical power equipment is often colour coded – 110 volt (yellow), 240 volt (blue) and 415 volt (red).

F
23

☑ When assembling a mobile tower scaffold, overhead electrical cables must be treated as live until it is proved that they are dead.

☑ No-one must start work near to exposed electrical conductors unless they are known to be dead. Damaged cables must be isolated or replaced.

☑ The padlock to an electrical lock-out guard can be fitted by anyone working on the equipment.

☑ If the mains isolator for a piece of equipment is found switched off upon arrival on site, work must not start until the person in control of the premises has been consulted.

☑ There must be adequate task lighting, where there is insufficient natural light to enable any job to be carried out safely.

Emergency situations

You may find that you are first on the scene following an accident to another worker, and it is important that you know what to do. If you find anyone who is obviously injured:

☑ make sure that you are not in any danger

☑ stay with the victim, keep them still and send someone else to find a first aider.

It is most important that everyone on site knows what to do in an emergency situation. A serious emergency may result in the evacuation of the whole site.

☑ If a natural gas leak in an enclosed area is reported, the area should be ventilated and the gas emergency service should be telephoned.

☑ If a refrigerant leak in an enclosed area is reported:
- the area must be ventilated
- all naked flames must be extinguished
- it must be established whether or not it is safe to enter the area before anyone attempts to do so.

Health risks

Health risk are often overlooked because the symptoms are not often immediately obvious and are slow to show. Examples of health risks that may have to be managed are listed below.

☑ Asbestos is likely to be found in any building built before the year 2000.

☑ Anyone who is likely to disturb asbestos should be trained and training must be appropriate to the work being undertaken.

☑ Anyone who is likely to disturb the fabric of a building must be aware that:
- asbestos could be present
- asbestos can be found in many places
- products include insulation boards around radiators, gaskets and seals in joints and rope seals in a boiler
- if the presence of asbestos is suspected, work must stop immediately and the situation must be reported to a supervisor or manager
- if asbestos exists, the asbestos register must be consulted before work starts.

☑ Anyone suffering from headache or sickness whilst using a solvent-based product (such as adhesive) should be taken into fresh air and made to rest as soon as possible.

☑ Discarded items of drug-using equipment must be safely removed by wearing gloves and using grips if practical. The supervisor or manager must be informed.

☑ Manual handling must be carried out in a way that avoids injury, such as:

 – generally assessing the task as a whole before attempting to lift items that are known to be heavy (such as rolls of lead)

 – operatives informing their supervisor and requesting assistance if required to move any load that they know is too heavy for them to move without assistance

 – using a suitable manual handling aid, (such as a trolley) if required, to move a heavy load, particularly over long distances.

☑ Repeatedly bending copper tube using an internal spring could result in long-term damage to the knees.

☑ Noise assessments must be carried out by a competent person where there is a danger of noise-related hearing loss.

☑ When carrying out solvent welding on plastic ductwork it is essential that the area remains well ventilated.

☑ The risks to health from working with lead can be avoided by:

 – preventing it from getting into the bloodstream by washing the hands after handling it

 – not smoking whilst bossing or otherwise handling it.

☑ The potentially fatal risks from legionella can be avoided by being aware that:

 – the bacteria is spread to humans though breathing in water droplets in the form of fine mists and sprays

 – suitable RPE with a protection factor of 40 must be worn when breaking into the system if exposure to sprays or mists cannot be prevented

 – the ideal temperature range for the bacteria to breed is between 20°C and 45°C

 – breeding grounds for legionella include slow-moving or stationary water supplies (such as infrequently used shower heads or 'dead legs') that are within the above temperature range

 – if an outbreak of legionella is suspected, the Health and Safety Executive must be informed.

LPG and other gases

LPG is a flammable and explosive gas that is often found on construction sites. Many other bottled gases are dangerous if not handled and stored properly because they are explosive and are stored at high pressure. Some safety precautions are:

☑ LPG cylinders that supply site cabins must be located outside the cabin

☑ LPG and acetylene cylinders must be stored in the open air to prevent the build-up of leaking gas

☑ if LPG bottles are transported and/or stored overnight in a van, there must be a low-level drainage route to the outside to protect against the accumulation of leaking LPG

F
23

☑ where LPG cylinders are being transported in a van they must be carried in a purpose-built container inside the vehicle

☑ anyone who has to transport more than 5 kg of LPG in a covered van must be trained and competent in the hazards relating to the gases

☑ it is important to know the difference between equipment that is used on propane and butane because propane equipment works on a higher pressure

☑ LPG is heavier than air and leaking gas will collect at the lowest point it can reach, (such as basements, drains or gulleys). Avoid such features when using or storing LPG

☑ except for cylinders designed for use on gas-powered forklift trucks, store all LPG cylinders in an upright position to prevent the liquid gas being drawn from the cylinder creating a hazardous situation

☑ if a leak is suspected in any part of an LPG system attempts to trace it must only be made using a proper leak detection fluid

☑ oxygen cylinders must be handled with great care due to the extremely high pressure to which they are filled

☑ when using oxyacetylene equipment:
  – the bottles must be secured in an upright position
  – the cylinders, hoses and flashback arrestors must be in good condition
  – the area must be well ventilated and clear of any obstructions
  – the bottles must be stored separate from other gas bottles in a special compound
  – green tinted goggles manufactured to BS EN 169:2002 must be worn by the person using the equipment
  – it should not be used for jointing copper tube using capillary soldered fittings,
  – it should not be used for fitting capillary soldered fittings to copper tubing

☑ acetylene cylinders must also be stored away from other gases, outside in a special storage compound

☑ it is important to be able to identify the content of gas cylinders by their colour. For this reason they are colour coded:
  – propane cylinders are red or orange
  – acetylene cylinders are maroon

☑ where welding is being carried out, screens must be provided to protect others from welding flash.

Lifting operations

Lifting operations have been the cause of many accidents because they were not properly planned, carried out or defective equipment was used. Everyone involved in planning lifting operations must be aware that:

☑ the sequence of operations in any lifting activity must be laid out in advance in a method statement (sometimes called a lifting plan)

☑ the safe working load (SWL) of any piece of lifting equipment or accessory must never be exceeded

F
23

☑ every piece of lifting equipment and each lifting accessory must be marked with their SWL

☑ if any item of lifting equipment is found to be defective the equipment must not be used and the problem must be reported to a supervisor or manager

☑ if any item of lifting equipment is found to be buckling whilst in use, the load must be lowered until the strain is released from the hoisting cable

☑ all items must be stable and secure whilst being lifted

☑ items that are lifted into a place where they will be installed must not be released from the hoist until securely fixed in place.

Personal protective equipment (PPE)

Wearing the correct personal protective equipment (PPE) can prevent exposure to harmful substances. The wrong type of PPE is likely to be useless. Always use the correct PPE, where a risk cannot be controlled by other measures, such as wearing:

☑ impact and dust resistant eye protection when drilling, cutting or grinding any material that could generate flying debris

☑ thermally protective gloves to avoid direct skin contact with pipe-freezing equipment and always read the COSHH assessment for the product

☑ a safety helmet, protective footwear, hearing protection, a face mask and eye protection when using a hammer drill

☑ ear defenders if working in a noisy environment or doing any job in which high levels of noise are generated (such as breaking up a cast iron bath)

☑ green-tinted goggles if carrying out oxyacetylene welding

☑ safety gloves, a face mask and eye protection if having to handle fibreglass roof insulation

☑ respiratory protective equipment (RPE) when using hazardous substances that can be breathed in. Do not start work if this hasn't been provided

☑ cut-resistant gloves when handling anything with sharp edges.

Safe methods of work

The importance of adopting safe methods of work, derived from carrying out a risk assessment and often specified in a method statement, cannot be overstated, for example:

☑ the correct hand tools must be used for any job (such as using a hammer and bolster chisel for taking up floorboards)

☑ the transportation of tools and materials must be carried out in a safe and responsible manner, such as:
  − carrying long lengths of tubing in a pipe-rack attached to the roof of a van
  − fixing a ladder to the roof rack of a van using proper ladder-clamps

☑ the exhaust fumes from vehicle exhausts are toxic; if engine-driven plant has to be run inside a building, the exhaust fumes must be extracted to a position outside the building

☑ liquid spills can be a slipping hazard, so inform a supervisor and keep people out of the area until they are cleaned up

F
23

☑ prevent contact with moving parts of machinery or rotating materials by enclosing them with guards or barriers

☑ be aware of sharp edges when using hand tools to cut through sheet material or pipes

☑ keep non-involved people out of the area when pressure testing pipework or vessels

☑ prevent the entanglement of clothing when using an electrically-powered threading machine

☑ a permit to work system should be introduced for all high risk work activities

☑ before starting work on any piece of equipment it is essential that the operation and maintenance manual for the equipment is consulted

☑ if someone is going to be working alone, to protect their safety they must:

   – register their presence with the site representative before starting work

   – ensure that arrangements are made for someone to periodically check that they are OK

☑ to prevent unauthorised access to plant and switchgear rooms the doors must always be kept locked

☑ no task should be carried out in an improvised manner using the wrong tool for the job. Anyone in this situation must wait for the correct tool to become available

☑ where possible lone working should be avoided. If it is necessary a system of periodically checking on the lone worker must be in place.

Working at height

Examples of good practice for safe working at height are:

☑ a risk assessment must have been carried out

☑ each ladder should be secured to the structure against which it is resting to prevent it slipping, ideally by lashing one of the upper rungs/styles to the structure

☑ when using a stepladder, the restraining mechanism, must be fully extended

☑ stepladders must only be used:

   – if a risk assessment shows they are suitable for the job

   – they are in good condition

   – for light, short-term work (lasting no more than a few minutes) and that does not involve stretching

☑ when a mobile tower scaffold is used, generally, only one working platform should be occupied at any one time

☑ when deciding the maximum height to which a mobile tower scaffold may be built the manufacturer's instructions must be referred to

☑ the hatch of a mobile access tower working platform must be closed immediately after gaining access to the platform

☑ before moving a mobile tower, all people, tools and equipment must be removed from the working platform

**F
23**

- ☑ the users of mobile tower scaffolds must be aware of the proximity of overhead live electric cables before erecting the tower

- ☑ edge protection must be fitted to working platforms to prevent the fall of a person or object, where this could result in injury or damage

- ☑ a stable working platform (such as a mobile tower scaffold) should be used for jobs where there is a good floor surface and 'heavier' type work is to be carried out at height

- ☑ if working near the edge of a flat roof that has a low parapet, edge protection consisting of double guard-rails and a toe-board must be installed at the roof edge

- ☑ ladders used on site must be labelled 'Class 1' (industrial) or 'BS EN 131'; any ladder labelled 'Class 2' (light trade) or 'Class 3' (domestic use only) must not be used

- ☑ wooden ladders that have been painted must not be used because the paint can hide defects

- ☑ all shafts, pits, service ducts, large floor voids and so on, must be fitted with double guard-rails and toe-boards or secure cover where someone could fall into them

- ☑ if working at height to dismantle lengths of soil pipe, it can be safely carried out by working in pairs and breaking the length at the collar to remove complete sections

- ☑ flue liners must be installed in a safe manner by working in pairs at roof level and using a safe method of access (such as a chimney scaffold or roof ladders)

- ☑ falling objects must be prevented when working above occupied areas

- ☑ as far as practical, access to ceiling voids or soffits containing a large number of services should be restricted. Alternative means of access may be required

- ☑ never use existing services as a make-shift working platform or a means of access.

F
23

Domestic heating and plumbing services (HAPS)

Installing or maintaining heating and plumbing services can present the risk of injury or ill health. Some examples of good practice are:

☑ temporary continuity bonding should be carried out before removing and replacing sections of metallic pipework to provide a continuous earth for the pipework installation

☑ when working where welding is being carried out, a screen should be provided to protect you from 'welding flash'

☑ the most likely risk of injury when cutting a pipe with hand-operated pipe cutters is because the inside edge of the cut pipe becomes extremely sharp to touch

☑ when transporting long lengths of pipe by van use a pipe rack fixed to the roof of the van. Similarly ladder clamps should be used to secure a ladder or stepladders to the roof rack of a van

☑ when taking up a length of floorboard to install pipework you should use a hammer and bolster (and not a hammer with a chisel or screwdriver).

If a job needs involves work below a ground-level suspended timber floor, you should first check or ask if the work could be performed from outside it, rather than entering a confined space.

Pipefitting and welding (industrial and commercial PFW)

Pipefitting and welding can present the risk of injury or ill health to you and others. Some examples of good practice are:

☑ when using a pipe threading machine a safety barrier should be erected around the whole length of the pipe and you should ensure your clothing cannot get caught on rotating parts of the machine

☑ when a new piece of plant has been installed but has not been commissioned, it should be left with all valves and switches 'locked off'

☑ before using oxyacetylene equipment it is essential to check:

    – the cylinders, hoses and flashback arresters are in good condition

    – the area is well ventilated and clear of any obstructions

☑ acetylene cylinders (maroon in colour) should be stored outside in a special storage compound when not in use

☑ when using oxyacetylene brazing equipment, the bottles should be stood upright and secured, preferably on a purpose made trolley

☑ when using pipe-freezing equipment to isolate the damaged section of pipe, you should wear gloves to avoid direct contact with the skin and read the COSHH assessment.

Only those involved in carrying out the pressure testing of pipework or vessels should be present.

F
23

Ductwork (DUCT)

Ductwork installation and maintenance

Installing or maintaining ductwork can present the risk of injury or ill health. Some examples of good practice are:

☑ if dismantling waste-extract ductwork, before starting the job it is essential to find out what the ductwork may be contaminated with

☑ before painting the external surface of any ductwork, the COSHH assessment for the paint should be read

☑ fume extraction must be provided when welding galvanised ductwork

☑ after using a solvent-based adhesive on ductwork:

- the ductwork must be left with the inspection covers off

- 'no smoking' signs must be displayed

- the area must be well ventilated

☑ if prior to fitting, a defect is noticed in any component of a system that is being installed, the item must not be fitted and a supervisor or manager must be informed

☑ before using a cleaning agent or biocide on a ductwork system:

- advice on the properties of the cleaning agent or biocide must be obtained from the manufacturer

- those doing the work must read the COSHH assessment for the cleaning agent or biocide

- an assessment of the risks of using the cleaning agent or biocide must be made

- a method statement for the work must be prepared

- the building occupier must be consulted

☑ before cleaning a system in an industrial laboratory or other premises where harmful particulates might be encountered:

- the system must be inspected

- samples must be collected from the system

- a job-specific risk assessment and method statement must be prepared

☑ if it is necessary for a person to enter ductwork, two of the factors that must be considered are the:

- dangers of working in confined spaces

- strength of the ductwork and its supports

☑ before working on a kitchen extraction system, the nature of the cooking deposits in the system should be established

☑ aluminium ductwork that has been pre-insulated with fibreglass must only be cut using tin snips with the person doing the cutting wearing RPE suitable for protecting against airborne fibres

☑ when jointing plastic-coated metal ductwork, welding presents far greater health risks than, for example, riveting, taping or using nuts and bolts.

F
23

Refrigeration and air conditioning (RAAC)

Refrigerants and other gases

Most gases have the potential to cause harm because they are explosive, stored at high pressure, are at very low temperatures or are harmful to the environment. Examples of good practice and the unsafe properties of gases are shown below.

☑ When not is use, refrigerant cylinders must be stored in a special, locked storage compound located in the open air.

☑ Refrigerant gases are heavier than air and if released into an enclosed space will sink to the lowest place they can seep into.

☑ If transported in a van, refrigerant bottles must be carried in a purpose-built container inside the vehicle.

☑ Flashback arrestors must be fitted between pipes and gauges of oxy-propane brazing equipment.

☑ When handling refrigerant gases, eye protection, overalls, thermal resistant gloves and safety boots must be worn.

☑ Oxygen must never be used for pressure testing because it could react with the oil in the compressor causing an explosion possibly resulting in serious injury or death.

☑ When pressure testing using nitrogen it is essential to ensure that:
   – the gauges can take the pressure required
   – the nitrogen bottle is secured in an upright position.

Safe methods of work

☑ Before entering a cold-room it must be established that the exit door is fitted with an internal handle.

☑ When a refrigerant leak has been reported in a closed area, it must be established that it is safe to enter before anyone attempts to do so.

Services and facilities maintenance (SAF)

Checking, installing, testing and commissioning installations

Where new plant or equipment is being installed it must be done in a manner that avoids injury to the people doing the job or anyone else. This must include ensuring that the plant or equipment cannot be operated in an unauthorised manner before it has been commissioned and handed over.

☑ The health and safety file for any building, where one has been compiled, is a possible useful source of information on the safe way of maintaining the systems within it.

☑ In a normal office environment, the temperature of the hot water at the tap furthest from the boiler should be at least 50°C within one minute of starting to run it.

☑ The maximum temperature of a cold water supply must be 20°C within two minutes of starting to run it.

☑ Two examples of a pressure system are:
  – medium and high temperature hot water systems above 95°C
  – steam systems.

☑ A written scheme of examination must be in place before a pressure system is operated.

☑ Where there is a cooling tower on site, it must have a formal log book that is kept up to date.

☑ On cooling tower systems the water must be chemically treated.

☑ When replacing the filters in an air-conditioning system:
  – a job-specific risk assessment and method statement must be prepared and followed
  – the person(s) doing the job must wear appropriate overalls and a respirator.

☑ After a gas boiler has been serviced it must be checked for:
  – flueing
  – ventilation
  – gas rate
  – safe functioning.

☑ Before adding an inhibitor to a heating system, the COSHH assessment for the product must be read and understood.

F
23

Further information

Glossary

Many words and terms that you will hear on a construction site are explained in the main part of this book. The list below includes some more terms that you might come across.

Adhesive. A substance used for sticking things together.

Abrasive wheel machine. A machine, such as a bench-mounted grinder or a disc-cutter, which is used for cutting or grinding materials.

Allergy. A damaging reaction of the body caused by contact with a particular substance.

Asbestos. A naturally occurring, heat-resistant substance that was once used extensively in construction work. Breathing in asbestos particles is harmful to the lungs.

Asthma. An illness that causes difficulty in breathing.

Bacteria. Germs that can cause some illnesses.

Barrier cream. A protective cream applied to your hands before starting work.

Bracing. Scaffold poles that make a scaffold rigid.

Brick-guard. A metal mesh fitted to a scaffold to prevent anything from falling through the gaps between the guard-rails and toe-board.

Cable ramp. A temporary 'hump' laid over a trailing cable to protect it from damage by people or traffic passing over it.

CCTV. Closed circuit television.

Cherry picker. A type of MEWP on which a passenger-carrying basket is located on the end of an articulating or extending arm.

COSHH. Control of Substances Hazardous to Health Regulations.

Crawling boards. A working platform or staging that allows access on a fragile roof.

Crush injuries. Injuries caused by something crushing a part of the body.

Distribution system (electrical). The method that is used to get electrical supplies to where they are needed on site.

Double-handling. Having to move something twice.

Edge protection. A framework of scaffold poles and scaffold boards erected around a sloping roof to stop anything falling over the edge.

Employee. Someone who works for someone else.

Employer. Someone who has people working for him or her.

HAVS. Hand-arm vibration syndrome.

Health and Safety at Work Act 1974. The main piece of health and safety law.

HFL. Highly flammable liquids.

HSE. Health and Safety Executive.

HSE inspector. An official who can inspect the site and take action if work is not being carried out safely.

Lanyard. A length of fabric that connects a safety harness with a fixed strong-point.

Ligament. A band of tough body tissue that connects bones or cartilage.

LPG. Liquefied petroleum gas.

MEWP. Mobile elevating work platform.

PAT. Portable appliance testing.

PPE. Personal protective equipment.

RCD. Residual current device.

RPE. Respiratory protective equipment.

Scissor lift. A type of MEWP with a platform that rises vertically.

Slewing. A part of an item of plant (such as the jib and counter-weight of a crane), rotating about a vertical axis.

Solvent. Chemical used to dissolve or dilute other substances.

Tripping hazard. Items lying around that you might trip over.

Ventilated. Supplied with fresh air.

Training record

Name of company _____

Name of employee _____

Name of supervisor _____

Instructions to supervisor

The employee and supervisor should sign each area of training listed below as it is completed and tick the box. The manager responsible should endorse the record and ensure that a copy is retained on file.

		Completed	Supervisor's signature
1	General responsibilities	☐	_____
2	Accident reporting and recording	☐	_____
3	Emergency procedures and first aid	☐	_____
4	Health and welfare	☐	_____
5	Personal protective equipment	☐	_____
6	Dust and fumes (Respiratory risks)	☐	_____
7	Noise and vibration	☐	_____
8	Hazardous substances	☐	_____

Completed   Supervisor's signature

9   Manual handling ☐

10   Safety signs and signals ☐

11   Fire prevention and control ☐

12   Electrical safety and hand-held tools and equipment ☐

13   Site transport safety ☐

14   Working at height ☐

15   Excavations and confined spaces ☐

16   Environmental awareness and waste control ☐

17   Demolition ☐

18   Plumbing or gas ☐

19   Highway works ☐

20   Specialist work at height ☐

21   Lifts and escalators ☐

22   Tunnelling ☐

23   Heating, ventilation, air conditioning and refrigeration (HVACR) ☐

I confirm that the named person has completed the training as listed:

I confirm that I have received the training as listed:

Signed _____   **Date** _____